Designing Courses
and Obstacles

Designing Courses and Obstacles

Pamela Carruthers
George H. Morris
Chrystine Jones Hogan
Bill Thomson

EDITED BY JOHN H. FRITZ

Houghton Mifflin Company Boston

1978

Library of Congress Cataloging in Publication Data

Main entry under title:
Designing courses and obstacles.
1. Courses (Horse sports) — Design and
construction. I. Carruthers, Pamela.
II. Fritz, John H., 1924–
SF294.35.D47   798′.45   78-2330
ISBN 0-395-26304-2
ISBN 0-395-26686-6 pbk.

Printed in the United States of America

H 10 9 8 7 6 5 4 3 2 1

Contents

Introduction · JOHN H. FRITZ   vii

Show Jumping Courses · PAMELA CARRUTHERS   1

Equitation Courses · GEORGE H. MORRIS   33

Courses for Hunters · CHRYSTINE JONES HOGAN   69

Courses for Three-Day Events · BILL THOMSON   99

A Final Note from the Editor   155

Conversion Table of Yards, Feet, and Meters   163

Introduction

DURING THE PAST twenty-five years interest in horses and the sports connected with them has grown at an amazingly rapid pace in the United States and in other parts of the English-speaking world. Activities that were once associated with a limited few in society have become commonplace. Each year sees the horse shows, combined events, and other forms of equestrian competition growing in numbers.

Not only has interest increased, so have the standards of performance improved year after year. The quality of the average horse seen in competition today is very high, and the number of quality riders is ever on the increase. In addition, the costs of showing have increased markedly in recent years, and competitors today expect the highest standards at the competitions they return to year after year.

In particular, competitors have come to expect that the courses at jumper, hunter, equitation, and combined training competitions be well thought out and well built to provide the best of competition. Good courses are essential to good competition. A good course, whether it be a test of jumpers, hunters, equitation riders, or eventers, should provide the competitor with a fair opportunity to demonstrate his and his horse's capacities and training. To quote from the rule book of the American Horse Shows Association, the national equestrian federation of the United States, "The good course should enable the capable, carefully schooled horse and the skillful rider to demonstrate their superiority; by the same token it should penalize the horse [and rider] of freakish or mediocre talent, the rogue, and the entry 'out of control.' " In combined training events, the cross-country course must be a good test of the horse's speed, endurance, and jumping ability, a test of the boldness of the horse, and a test of the ability of the rider to control his horse and to prepare his horse for the situations encountered. Courses must also be geared to the level of competition offered so as not to overface the novice horse and/or rider on the one hand yet be a true test of ability at the advanced or open level.

The growing demand for good competitive courses has been recognized by the American Horse Shows Association, which, beginning in 1977, requires recognized shows to designate in their prize list and catalogue the person or persons responsible for the design and construction of the courses. The larger and more important shows and events use professional course designers to ensure the quality of their courses. But such people are limited in number and are beyond the means of the average show or event. Yet the desire to have good courses is found everywhere, and one again and again hears the cry for guidance for those who are designing and building courses. In recent years, the United States Equestrian Team (USET), the American Horse Shows Association, and the United States Combined Training Association have all sponsored seminars and clinics on course design and construction, which have been well attended. But even these efforts have not met the growing demand for guidance and direction. Thus the reason for this book.

The book is first of all aimed at those who are currently designing and building courses at horse shows or combined training events but whose knowledge and ability are limited. It is next directed at those who have been wanting to get into course design but are not sure whether their knowledge of the subject is adequate or not. It is also for show managers and committees who need to know what makes a course a good course and the importance of good courses to the success of their show and event so that competitors will want to return another time. And it is finally aimed at riders and trainers who need to better understand what is involved in a good course and what good courses seek to bring out in the training and ability of horses and riders, in order that they may better prepare and train for successful competition.

The four experts who have contributed to this book are all internationally known in their respective fields. Pamela Carruthers has in recent years designed the show jumping courses for almost every major competition in the United States and Canada, as well as for important events in England and Europe. She is one of a handful of course designers called upon when an important national or international competition is being held. Bill Thomson has not only been the designer and builder of the courses at Burghley, in England, for the past decade and more, he is the British Horse Society's chief expert to assist organizers of horse trials and three-day events with their courses, and he has designed courses in the United States and Canada. George Morris, a former rider on the United States Equestrian Team, is one of the most successful teachers and trainers in the United States today. His equitation students regularly place highly in the finals of the Medal and the Maclay, and students and horses trained by him are seen again and again among the champions at major shows. Chrystine Jones Hogan, also a former rider with the USET, an active trainer and teacher, is one of a growing number of professional course designers employed by major shows to create the best of hunter and jumper competitions.

These experts have clearly set forth the aims and purposes of the particular equestrian sport they are discussing. They also explain what makes a course and a fence a good course and a good fence in terms of those aims and purposes. All emphasize the importance of planning, the need for variety, and the difference between a course or fence that is challenging and one that is gimmicky and unfair. They also have some useful advice to the rider and trainer on how to train for major competitions today in order to be among those in the winner's circle.

Well illustrated with figures and photographs, this book will, we hope, fulfill the demand for a reliable guide to a subject more and more people are becoming interested in.

JOHN H. FRITZ

Morristown, New Jersey

Show Jumping Courses

PAMELA CARRUTHERS

Pamela Carruthers. Pamela Carruthers is one of the world's leading international designers of show jumping courses. She is a native of Chippenham, England, where she began riding at the age of five. At fifteen she went to school in France, where she rode some of the leading French show jumpers of the day and developed a deep interest in the design and construction of jumper courses. During the 1950s she rode with the British Show Jumping Team.

Mrs. Carruthers has been designing jumper and hunter courses for over twenty years and took on her first assignment at a major show some eighteen years ago. She is the course designer at Hickstead, in England, probably the finest permanent jumping arena in the world, and in addition to Great Britain, she has designed courses at major competitions in Australia, Canada, France, Iran, Mexico, the Netherlands, South Africa, and the United States. Included among the international competitions for which she has one or more times designed the courses are the European Men's, Ladies', and Junior Championships, the Men's and Ladies' World Championships, the Washington International, the National in New York, the Royal Winter Fair in Toronto, the South Africa Jumping Derby, and the Masters in Calgary, Alberta. She has written articles on course design for the *Chronicle of the Horse, Practical Horseman,* and *Horse and Hound.*

Introduction

Designing show jumping courses is a very interesting and responsible job, but don't let this frighten you away if you are a beginner. Everyone can start at small shows and even at home. It is only possible for me to lay down guidelines for people to work on, for it is only by actual experience in designing courses and watching the result that you can learn and eventually produce your own style. Obviously some people have more time to do their preparation beforehand and to work at shows, and it is these people who will eventually become the really top course designers. But there are many smaller shows where people who haven't so much time can still play a very useful role and get satisfaction from helping to bring on young horses and riders.

If you want to become a course designer, my advice is to spend time working on your own, while at the same time going to the bigger shows and watching carefully. If possible, ask whether you can act as an assistant. Do this with as many people as possible, as all the top designers have slightly different ideas, and you must learn to take what you decide is the best from each one.

One of the most difficult problems for a newcomer is that many of the riders will come and ask you to alter this or that on your course. Some may have genuine and sensible requests, but others may want a change to suit their particular horse. To begin with, make the courses simple and try not to do anything that will cause controversy, so that you know it is not necessary to make any changes. Later on, when you know the competitors better, you will learn from whom to expect advice. Remember, above all, that everyone makes mistakes, sometimes for reasons beyond one's control. When you make them, admit them, and the riders will learn to respect you for doing so.

Aims of Course Design

What are the aims of the course designer? One is to design courses that make a good public spectacle. Although this is not as important at small shows as at large ones, so much of what you do to achieve this will apply to your other aims that it is a good idea to start thinking of this from the outset, while naturally remembering that the horses and riders are also the most important.

Another aim is to design a course that flows; one in which the riders don't have to keep checking their horses, yet which does not produce too many clear rounds; one in which the faults are well spread out over the whole course but leave enough competitors at the end to make an exciting jump-off. This is what the public enjoys. The fences must be built to make the course as varied as possible, and the colors must be blended harmoniously. In fact, the arena should have the appearance of the countryside brought into a small area, and when I say "small," I mean that an outdoor arena should at a minimum be 300 feet by 250 feet.

Show jumping is a very exciting spectacle and should be presented to the public as such. Naturally many of the large novice or preliminary classes become boring, but the open competitions in the United States, as in Britain, are now as good as any in the world. These should be put on at a time when the public will watch. If they can be educated to enjoy horse shows, their participation will help to bring down the high entry fees that are essential to make a show pay its way at the moment. Luckily, everything that I consider goes to make a show a crowd pleaser also applies to my aim as far as horses and riders are concerned. One can hope they will all be going as well or better at the end of the show. Well-built fences and free-flowing tracks all help to produce this result.

The final aim is to keep to the timetable of the show management, hoping that this has been worked out realistically. If the time allowed for a class is too short, the course designer may be forced into using trick fences or distances to cut down the clear rounds, and immediately all his aims are at risk. I am sure the public doesn't enjoy horses and riders being tricked into making faults; and when the courses are tricky, horses and riders start losing confidence in each other and the course designer, and the show will end on an unhappy note. It is essential in planning for a class to allow two minutes per horse in the original class plus time for the jump-off, for changing the course, and for walking it before the jump-off.

Planning a Course

To fulfill his aims, the course designer needs to know the size of the arena and the position of any permanent fences. He also needs to know where the judge will be sitting, so that both the start and the finish are not completely at the other end of the arena, which means that a lot of cable will be needed if an electric timer is used, or there will be a long walk for the timer if timing is done by hand. He should know where the entrance and the exit to the arena are, and naturally, if there are going to be public stands, he should design the course to give them the best view. The course designer needs to know the timetable of the show, so that no time is wasted changing from one competition to another. It is also a great help to have a list of the fence material, as it is always better to have a short, well-built course, even using fences twice, than a long one with airy fences lacking in filling material.

Once we know our aims, the size of the arena, the fences available, and the competition to be planned for, what steps do we follow to obtain a good result? First, there is the track you are going to ask the horse to follow; second, the type and position of the fences you are going to use; and third, and possibly most important, the distance between each fence.

I much prefer working outside in a fairly large arena. I think it gives a course designer a great deal more opportunity for variety in the track and in the use of fences and distances. At the same time, I think it is good and interesting to design both indoor and outdoor courses.

Let me first tell you how I plan a one-day show, for if you are starting out as a course designer this is probably what you will be doing. I decide which is the big competition of the day and work on the track for this. If there are going to be no experienced horses, I will use a simple figure-eight type course, with at least two changes of direction. If the open class has some good horses, I can be a little more imaginative. But do remember that some courses are not good because the designer has tried to be too clever. I know that most of my failures have come from this.

I always work on graph paper when doing my course plans. Working outdoors, I use 1 inch to represent 10 yards, and working indoors, to represent 10 feet. In fact, working outdoors I always talk of distances in yards except in combination fences. This is assuming that your arena is a minimum of 300 feet by 250 feet. If it is less than this, I consider you have to use the type of course that you would have for an indoor show. In a very big arena I would use ½ inch to represent 10 yards, as when working you do not want to handle a very large, unwieldy plan. It is a complete fallacy to believe that you need a small arena to shorten the courses. In a fair-sized arena you need fewer complete changes of direction (each time you get to the end of the arena it just about doubles the distance used between fences).

Now, having got my graph paper, I draw in the exact size of the arena and mark in any permanent obstacles or trees, the exit and entrance to the arena, the position where the judge(s) will be, and, for my own benefit, the main spectator stand. I always draw my plans so they will appear correct from where the judge(s) is sitting. Having been a judge myself, I know that at the end of a long day I find it very trying to work from a plan that is upside down, and for the competitor, as long as the entrance is clearly marked, it should be no problem.

I always start by playing about with matchsticks to represent fences, and I work out the main competition first. I start with the matches because they are so easy to move around if I don't manage to find a good track for the jump-off. I prefer not to have the first fence too near the entrance, especially for novice or preliminary horses. But at a one-day show I don't want to cause the start and the finish to be moved too often, so the start may remain the same all day. Therefore, no one will start near the entrance. I thus work out a fairly simple track. When I have found one that will work if used in two or more courses, I draw the line of the track so as to be sure the turns are smooth on all courses. I then draw the lines for the fences, and number the different courses with different-colored ink, as I like to have a master plan to work from, both for when I draw out each separate course for competitors and judges, and for when I come to build the course.

I like to position an outdoor course for the whole day if possible, as much time is saved between competitions if fences don't have to be moved. I would also say that in doing this, you have to compromise slightly in that the jump-off in one course will turn out better than in another, as shown on page 7. But surprisingly, it isn't always the course you expect to be most successful that comes off the best.

The figures on pages 7 and 8 show a course that can be used for several classes. Twelve efforts are needed for the Open class. I have used the exact number of fences needed to fulfill the requirements. If you have enough material this is best, but you might have to use a plan where a fence is jumped twice. In this case, be sure that it isn't jumped too soon for a second time and never use it twice in the jump-off.

In this plan the start is not the same for all the courses (two courses have one start, two another), but the finish is the same in all. The disadvantage of this plan is that some of the fences have to be jumped in a

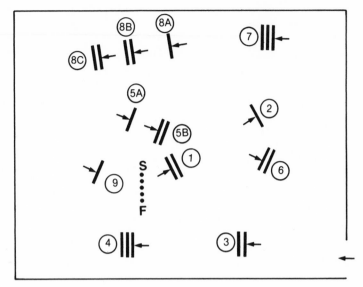

Jump off   1 • 2 • 3 • 4 • 5 • 8 • 9

Fig. 1.   Course for Open Jumper Class

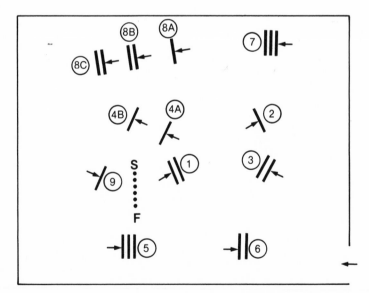

Jump off   1 • 2 • 3 • 4 • 5 • 8 • 9

Fig. 2.   Course for Amateur-Owner and Junior Jumper Classes

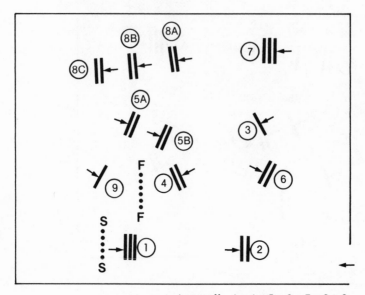

Fig. 3.   Course for Intermediate Jumper Class

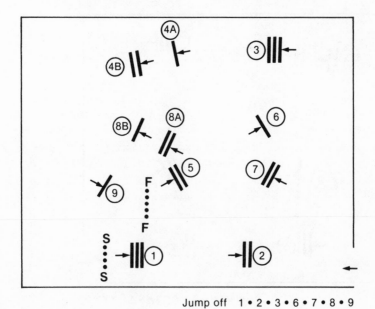

Jump off   1 • 2 • 3 • 6 • 7 • 8 • 9

Fig. 4.   Course for Preliminary Jumper Class

different direction in the various competitions, and precious time is taken up in altering the fences; or the fences have to be built so that they can be readily jumped in both directions.

There are actually four different ways to jump this course for ordinary AHSA Table II Section 2 competitions, and each of them has a jump-off that gives the rider the opportunity to gallop on in places and at the same time to show that his horse can turn and jump off a short stride.

After a spread fence in a jump-off, I don't like to ask a horse to turn back on his tracks, as I feel the horse is so often punished for a good jump over a wide fence by being pulled sharply round, especially by the less experienced rider. If the rider is going to be asked to turn back immediately on landing, or to turn through more than 90 degrees, then the fence before the turn should be an upright one so that it can be angled. I consider that the jump-off should flow just as freely as the first round. The jump-off is more important than the first round, as this is where the competition is won or lost, if the course designer hasn't made the course too stiff, resulting in only one clear round the first go. I feel a single clear round is permissible in an AHSA Table I class, where touches count, but never in a Table II class. In theory I don't like Table I classes, but in practice I do think they stop green horses being asked to jump too big fences too soon. At the same time, I feel the prize money for Table I classes should always be small, as I think overrapping causes a horse to lose his natural arc, and if riders want to win in a Table I class, they tend to do this. If a "touch" class is really more of a schooling class, as it should be, there is not the same incentive to win. A young horse can always win the money when he is ready, if he is good enough, in Table II classes.

Once we have worked out the track, the next thing is to consider the type of fences to be used. There are basically three types: (a) the straight or upright fence; (b) the parallel bar or oxer type, in which the front rail is either one hole lower in front — ascending parallel — or a true parallel (a more difficult fence), with back and front rails the same height; and (c) the staircase or triple bar type, which is sloping and is the easiest of the three. I would probably use the last for a first fence, especially for preliminary horses. I like the first fence to be a gift to the rider.

Now how am I going to use the other fences? A straight fence is generally more likely to be knocked down going toward home or downhill. Two spread fences followed by an upright one will very often present a bit of a problem. Also, I must remember that if a fence might be jumped at an angle in the jump-off, it is kinder to use a straight fence. An oxer or parallel fence is harder going away from home or uphill. A staircase is really only a problem going away from home if it is wide, and going toward home if followed by an upright fence at a good distance, so that the horse may become too much on the forehand and thus knock the upright fence down. You may well feel now that I intend to use fences to trick horses. I don't, but the course must be a problem that the horse and rider have to overcome, and the fences are one of my means of setting fair problems.

Let us now go round the course shown in the figures. In planning the fences for the Open course (Figure 1), remember: number 1 is a parallel, a perfectly fair fence for an Open class, but I would have it ascending, not square, and going toward the entrance; number 2 is an upright fence; 3, going away from home, an oxer; 4, a triple bar, followed by 5A and 5B (4A and 4B, Amateur-Owner/Junior classes; 8A and 8B Preliminary course). As this combination has to be jumped in different ways in the various courses, I have two alternatives, either two upright fences with one stride between or an upright in and an oxer out, or vice versa when jumped in the opposite direction, as in some of the courses shown in the figures. The distance between combination fences varies, depending on whether the upright or oxer comes first, by approximately 1 foot, and one can alter the spread depending on whether the oxer is the in or the out, as shown in Figure 5.

Fig. 5.   This illustration shows the need to re-set certain fences as a result of taking an in-and-out in different directions. In the Open class, where the oxer is the second fence, the distance is 24′9″ and the spread is 5′3″, while in the Preliminary class, where the oxer is the first fence, the spread is 4′6″ and the distance 25′6″. The only element that has to be moved is that marked *X*.

Why haven't I told you distances before type of fences? My distances depend on the type of fences I use, and as I am telling you this in the order in which I work, distances will have to wait. Fence number 6 is again an oxer, 7 is a triple bar. Number 8A is an upright with two strides to 8B, an oxer, then one stride to 8C, again an oxer, and the course finishes up with 9 as a straight fence. I have made the distance between 8A and 8B two strides as this becomes the first combination on the Preliminary course, which I want to be easy.

On my plan I may not decide whether to use ascending or square parallels until I know the caliber of the horses I have in a class. To make for variety I will have at least one square parallel, which would probably be fence 6 in the Open course. If I have good horses I will probably use more square parallels than ascending ones. I can't emphasize too strongly that though all the preparation must be done before the show, it is best to leave the final decisions as to height and spread until you know the caliber of the horses; a designer should be able to produce a good competition with moderate horses. If fences are well filled in and solid-looking, the standard of jumping is always better. But I don't approve of turning all the fences into staircases. This does nothing to improve the horses or riders, and the class will probably be won by the horse that can gallop the fastest.

Now that we have decided on the track and type of fence to be used, we come to the final means a course designer has of testing horse and rider, the distance used between fences. I assume that a horse's stride is 12 feet or 4 yards, so a simple multiple of 12 feet or 4 yards between fences works out pretty well. On outside courses I very rarely put fences closer than 28 yards apart. I find I can walk a distance pretty accurately, so if I use 28 yards or more between fences, I don't bother to measure with a tape, for in six or more horse strides, if I am out the odd foot, it will not matter. But for distances less than 28 yards, I always measure with a tape. When one considers distances, it is important to remember that any uphill approach shortens a horse's stride by 6 to 9 inches in a combination, and it also shortens the stride between fences, whereas a downhill approach can lengthen a horse's stride by up to 1 foot in combinations. Heavy going also shortens a horse's stride. The type of fence used causes one to use different distances in combinations, and I give on page 12 a list of suggested distances to be used with the different types of obstacles in combination.

Naturally these are only average distances on average going. People ask me, do I shorten these distances for preliminary horses, and on the whole my answer would be no. The object is to get preliminary horses jumping freely and boldly, so I would rather err on the long than the short side. With more experienced horses I do vary the distances I use in combinations. If I take the average distance between two upright fences as 26 feet, I could reduce it to 24 feet, which, over two big uprights, would be very difficult, or I could extend it to 28 feet, which would probably present very few problems. At the same time, if we take the example of 24 feet 6 inches between two ascending oxers, we could not reduce that by more than 6 inches. We could increase the distance at the most by 1 foot, but we could not use a wide spread in the second oxer.

In fact, I think this tells us that with an upright fence we can play about with the distances, but with a spread we must be much more care-

For Combination Obstacles the following are considered to be "true" distances for one or two strides between fences for the average open competition according to the type of obstacles included in the combination:

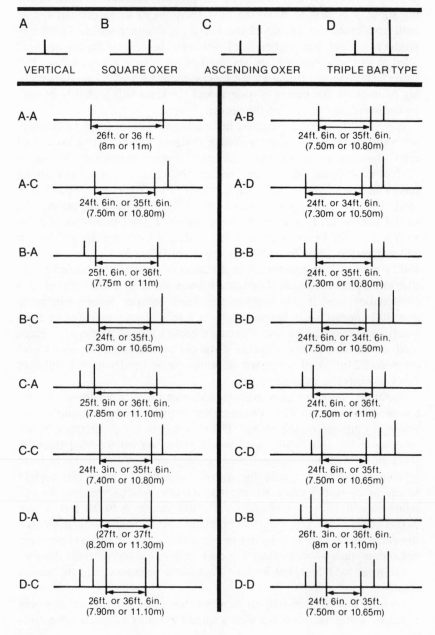

A	B	C	D
VERTICAL	SQUARE OXER	ASCENDING OXER	TRIPLE BAR TYPE

A-A
26ft. or 36 ft.
(8m or 11m)

A-B
24ft. 6in. or 35ft. 6in.
(7.50m or 10.80m)

A-C
24ft. 6in. or 35ft. 6in.
(7.50m or 10.80m)

A-D
24ft. or 34ft. 6in.
(7.30m or 10.50m)

B-A
25ft. 6in. or 36ft.
(7.75m or 11m)

B-B
24ft. or 35ft. 6in.
(7.30m or 10.80m)

B-C
24ft. or 35ft.)
(7.30m or 10.65m)

B-D
24ft. 6in. or 34ft. 6in.
(7.50m or 10.50m)

C-A
25ft. 9in or 36ft. 6in.
(7.85m or 11.10m)

C-B
24ft. 6in. or 36ft.
(7.50m or 11m)

C-C
24ft. 3in. or 35ft. 6in.
(7.40m or 10.80m)

C-D
24ft. 6in. or 35ft.
(7.50m or 10.65m)

D-A
(27ft. or 37ft.
(8.20m or 11.30m)

D-B
26ft. 3in. or 36ft. 6in.
(8m or 11.10m)

D-C
26ft. or 36ft. 6in.
(7.90m or 11.10m)

D-D
24ft. 6in. or 35ft.
(7.50m or 10.65m)

ful of doing so. Look at the chart above for distances in combination fences. Beyond combinations we can take the 12-foot stride as our guide for distances between fences, but it is wise to consider the type of fence used up to 72 feet. Using 12-foot strides, we will find that 48 feet is just right for upright to upright, but for triple bar to upright it would be too short, and for upright to triple bar it would be very long. The more strides between fences, the less the type of fence matters.

Many of the top riders like the designer to use distance problems because they can overcome them. But in my opinion, if used constantly, we find that the riders overcome them by checking their horses. The less experienced riders will then get their horses' heads in the air and the horses will jump with hollow backs and loss of freedom. When we use distance problems, we are really defeating our aim of improving the horses and riders. The top riders will overcome the problem, but the less experienced riders and horses will deteriorate. Therefore use distance problems with care.

Having discussed distances, let us put them in for the Open course in our first figure: Fences number 1 to number 2, 28 yards; number 3 to number 4, 32 yards; number 5A to number 5B, if two uprights, 26 feet, but if one is an upright and one an oxer, 24 feet 9 inches; number 7 to number 8A, 28 yards; number 8A to number 8B, 35 feet 6 inches; and number 8B to number 8C, 24 feet 3 inches. I will always leave at least 20 yards coming away from the turn, that is, at least 20 yards from the end of the arena to fence number 9, and if it is going to a combination such as number 5A, then I leave more room to get at it.

We now have the course plan with distances, type of fence, and position, so there only remains to work out the actual materials to be used.

Fence Material

Let us discuss fence material. First and foremost are the wing standards, uprights and pillars for supporting the rails. They must be solid and stand well on the ground. For most shows the plain wing standards are best, as these will nearly always stand up without pegging. Pillars generally need pegging, as, being solid, they have more wind resistance. As well as being solid, wing standards should have holes for cups to within 6 inches of the ground, and the inside upright should be flat so that the filling material, such as a wall or gate, does not have to be above or in front of a protruding foot. This is the disadvantage of four-legged uprights. They are not suitable for the front element of a fence, and when a spread fence has to be turned round, it is very time-consuming to have to change the standards. Three-legged uprights are good for big outdoor shows where there is plenty of labor and plenty of iron hooks to peg them down. Ordinary wing standards may be straight or sloping. The sloping ones are lighter, but the straight ones can have holes on both sides and can be turned round if one side is broken. I like the feet to be slotted where the upright part fits so that the upright is less inclined to swing. I also like the foot to have a half-moon cut out, as I find these stand better on uneven ground, as in Figure 6.

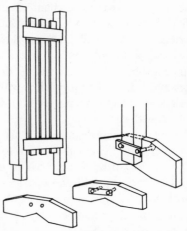

Fig. 6. Supports for Wing Standards

Next, we must consider cups. These must be solid. The actual holding part should have a depth of approximately one third of the diameter of the rails. I think gates, planks, ladders, and so on, should have shallower cups because anything heavier than a rail becomes dangerous in the cup depth ideal for rails, even when it is not used as the top element. Probably aluminum or plastic cups are the safest, as they have no sharp edges, but they are expensive, and since cups are always getting lost, it is just not economical to use them often. I would like to have available at least two depths of cups, and suggest they be painted different colors to be easily distinguished from each other.

Rails should be round, approximately 4 to 5 inches in diameter, and again, for general use, should be 12 feet long. And, to give variety and demand accuracy, they may be 8 feet long. Big outdoor shows want longer rails for wider fences.

Let us think of filling material. This must be constructed like a child's building set, so that each piece of material can be used in different ways. The filling is divided into two sorts — that which hangs, such as gates, ladders, panels, planks, and so on, all of which must be exactly the same length as the rails — and material that stands, such as small walls or brush fences. These should be built in at least two sections for easy carrying and should measure when complete no less than 6 inches smaller than the rails, so that they fit in easily between the uprights. Lastly, there are the extras, such as greenery and straw bales, which can be used in many ways to make a course look attractive. Care must be taken that when a fence is knocked down these fillings can be replaced exactly as they were, and that this can be done quickly.

Finally, we should consider colors. In a normal set of fences, there should be three or four different colors alternating with white, with at least twelve rails of each, plus rustic rails and gates. On the whole, a rustic fence is best kept rustic, and should also have rustic wing standards. Painted wing standards, I think, are best white and one other color. In a combination it looks much better if the same color wing standards are used all through. Though ideally these would tone with the rails, in a normal set of fences it really makes life much easier if the wing standards are all the same (except for rustic to go with rustic fences), as this saves a lot of time in building the course.

The walls should be of a color that will blend with other colors, with the gates mostly white or rustic. Ladders should be white, as they can then be used with any colors; and planks, like the rails, ought to be white and one other color. Most sets of fences have at least six white rails so that these can be used for hunter courses and in jumper courses as a variation.

Here is a list of material for a normal course:

4 pairs rustic wing standards
18 pairs colored wing standards
1 pair pillars with a 3-foot wall
1 pair pillars with a 16-inch wall
1 ordinary and 1 picket gate, 3.0 feet, white
1 ordinary and 1 picket gate, 2.0 feet, white
1 Fairfield gate, 2.0 feet
2 rustic gates, 2 feet, 6 inches
6 planks, red and white
4 ladders, white
36 colored rails (12 each red and white, green and white, black and white)
12 rustic rails
6 white rails
2 brush boxes, 2 feet 6 inches and 3 feet 6 inches, white

We can now work out the material for each fence. For my own use I put abbreviations on my master plan. For my helpers I have three different methods. Either I work it out with them and they write it on their own plans, or I write a postcard for each fence showing the exact material, a drawing done sideways, and the height and spread of that fence. This is good if you have plenty of help, as then two people can be given a fence to put up, and they can get on with it, and all you have to do is check that it is right when the course is up. The third method is to make up a detailed work sheet for the helpers.

Having done all this, there is some remaining homework, and I do beg people to do all this homework, as if it is well done beforehand, you can really concentrate on building the course when the time comes, and your helpers will bless you because you can work more quickly and accurately. Your remaining work is to draw out the separate course plans for the four different courses. I always do one plan of each and then get them photocopied with as many copies as I need for the judges, competitors, and helpers. There are two reasons for getting them copied: first, it saves time, and second, you know that everyone has the same plan. With hand-copying it is just too easy to make mistakes, especially in the jump-off fences. I know that competitors like a bigger plan on posterboard. To do this accurately takes a long time, and I have had too many slip-ups over jump-offs. No matter whether I or someone else has done the plan, the slip-ups occur. If the show likes a big plan I insist that one of the photocopied sheets be put up as well, and if there is a discrepancy, this is the one that counts.

I generally put a number indicating the order of the class in the schedule at the top left corner of the course sheet (this is for the ring crew and myself). Then across the top I add the class name and number, the type of horse it is for, the show name, the table of penalties, and the speed. At the bottom, the course distance, time allowed, jump-off fences, the jump-off distance, and the jump-off time if applicable are added. I draw in the lines for the fences as accurately as possible. I do not write in the distances, as it is up to the rider to walk the distances.

For international competitions we are supposed to mark the type of fence used. In this case I draw in one, two, or three lines to represent an upright, oxer, or staircase. Since this does rather confine your options, at small shows I probably only use one line with a direction arrow drawn through it. I do not draw any lines between fences on these plans, unless for safety reasons I wish this line to be followed, and if I do this, I write below and underline that the fixed line must be observed.

Building the Course

In order to set up the course I always like to get to the arena at least half an hour before I expect the ring crew to arrive. It is a help to have one person with you. First, I put out the numbers for the big competition, and then I like to lay out a rail of the right color where each fence is going. There may be some uneven places in the ring, and if the ring is large enough you will be able to make modifications in position and distance. If you do this before the ring is cluttered with material, it is easier to see what you want to do and exactly how all the courses will work out. If you wait to do this until you have the ring crew, you will have all of them asking what they are to do, and I find it more satisfactory to get the positioning done ahead of time. Naturally the rails are not exactly in position, for though I will walk the distances between fences and in combinations, I will only have guessed at the distance I need to add for spreads.

Thus, having laid the course out, when the ring crew arrives I get them to put the material out. I turn the numbers so that they can be seen from where the material is lying. I warn them that the fence is going where the rail is lying, and that they should put the material in such a way that the fence can be easily erected. I get all the wing standards out first, then the rails and filler material for each fence, and then give one person the job of putting round the cups, asking for two to each rail, gate, or plank. Some people start building the combination fences first, but having got my rails in position, I generally start at the first fence and work round the course. The upright fences I want to be true upright fences, and with the oxers I want the front face to be straight and not with brush or wall pulled out in front to turn it into a staircase. I want the fences to look solid and inviting, particularly the first fence of a combination, as I want the horse and rider to be able to attack these. For instance, in a double of uprights, if widely spaced rails are used for the first part and are followed by a wall, young horses will be discouraged; they will tend to look at the wall and not concentrate on the rails; whereas, constructed the other way round, it will be a really encouraging fence to jump.

When building doubles or trebles remember always to measure inside to inside: that is, between 8B and 8C of our sample course, for example, from the back rail of 8B to the front of 8C. The only exception of inside to inside is when the filler material sticks out at the back to form a hog's back type of fence, as shown in Figure 17. In this case, measure from

A.

B.

Fig. 7. Two Examples of Well-Constructed Triple Bar Step Fences. *A* illustrates the importance of using materials painted to blend together. Note how the flags are placed on the rear elements or how two sets of flags are used to avoid the problem of a horse that might jump through the wings. The fence in *B* consisting of brush and rails has a more natural appearance than that in *A*.

the top back rail, and when building combinations always measure inside from both sides.

The easiest way to build a combination of fences on a straight line is to put a stick in the middle of the first element, and if it is a three combination, line up on that. I generally use two-colored rails for actual positioning, as they are easier to center, even if I intend to use one color for the obstacle. I set the top rail of each fence in a combination, and then fill in when the fences are straight. Nothing is more annoying than having to move all the filler material if the combination is not lined up.

If you use a wall with bricks and then rails over the top, unless the rails are directly over the front edge of the wall, a true straight fence will not be formed, and if the bricks were knocked out it would be a fault. If the top bricks were rounded and you had the rails over the front edge, this would give a false ground line. So call the judge's attention to what you have done, and put the rails over the middle of the

A.

B.

Fig. 8. *A* illustrates an inviting oxer fence consisting of a white gate and rails. *B* clearly shows how, in such a fence, only one rail is used for the second element to avoid an accident in the case of a fall or a severe knockdown.

Fig. 9. An attractive fence consisting of pillars, wall, rails, and flowers and illustrating how filler elements such as walls should be less wide than the rails above them.

Fig. 10. *A* and *B* give two examples of nicely built rustic fences. Such fences are not only attractive but give variety to a course.

Fig. 11. *A, B,* and *C* show three fences that are airy and thus not inviting. Each could be easily improved by adding additional rails or flower boxes or other filler material to give a more definite ground line.

wall. Similarly, flowers should not stick out in front of the fence for the same reason. I never use a rail on the ground as a ground line as (a) it tends to get moved, and (b) if a horse refuses and puts his foot on the rail, it will roll and may cause an accident.

When the rails are being put up I always try and space them evenly to give the fence a good appearance, and if they are over a wall or brush, I don't like a big space between them and the wall. On oxers as a safety precaution I never put two rails on the back. On staircase fences where I only use two pairs of wing standards I do sometimes use two rails on the back, but I always put the lower rail four holes lower than the top one. I put the flags out last when the first course is set, and on spread fences I always put the flags to the back standards to avoid any trouble if the horse jumps through the wings.

Having set up the Open course, I now have to change this to the Preliminary course, changing the heights to the required specifications, and reducing the spreads. Fences 1 and 2 have to be jumped from the opposite direction to what it was in the Open, so I leave the standards and change the rails and filler material around. On fence 3, if I reduce the spread I do it from the front so that I leave the same distance between fences 3 and 4. When I alter the spread on 4B, I must pull the back in approximately 6 inches so as not to change the distance between 4A and 4B. I take all the material out and remove the cups from the last bit of the combination, but leave the wing standards in position for the later classes. I don't like to have wing standards at the approach to a combination as I think they distract the horse's attention, but provided the cups are removed, I don't think they matter at the far end of a double.

All spare rails that I will need for the Open class I leave at the side of the ring near the fence for which they will be needed. I now put the flags around. Check that the start and the finish are the correct distances from the first and the last fences.

Then see that the practice fences, at least one upright and one oxer, are put up in the warm-up area, and then have all the spare material stacked in the corner of the arena so that it is quick to get at in case of breakages. Always work out material so that there is at least one, and preferably two, spare rails of each color. You don't want to mix colors in the fences, but it doesn't matter for the practice fences.

Last, there are the different courses and jump-offs to measure. In Preliminary classes be really liberal in your measuring, but in the Open class the course should be measured in the track the horse is likely to follow. The corners must not be cut too short, as nothing is worse than a competition where the time allowed is too tight.

Fig. 12.   A water fence with a fence in the middle is a good fence for a Preliminary course in which you are introducing a novice horse to water. (Photo by Bespix.)

Fig. 13.   A permanent bank that can be jumped from all directions and that is large enough to be used in a variety of ways. (Photo by Bespix.)

Fig. 14.   Big Water Jump, Hickstead. This has a 24′ front. On the first day of a meeting it is generally used with a pole over it, as here. Thereafter it is jumped with only the brush or a flat take-off board. (Courtesy of Bespix.)

Having done all the essentials, it is time to try to improve the course with greenery. Use rubber buckets filled with dirt and any greenery stuck in, or, if buckets are not available, tie the green to the wing standards. For filling the fences, stick the greenery into straw bales. It is these final touches that make such a difference to the course. The whole effect is so much more pleasing for the riders and the public, and I am sure horses jump better over a well-presented, well-filled fence.

Show Day

Now the competitors have walked the course, and the first horse has come in. I always try and position myself near the center, having placed my ring crew in pairs and explained that while the first horse goes they should watch and wait until the end of the round unless there is a refusal. After that they will see when it is safe to go to a fence.

If the whole fence is knocked down, start building from the bottom. I have seen many squashed fingers when people put the top rails on first, which can fall as the lower ones are fitted underneath. When a rail falls, it is always easier and quicker for two people to put it up. In an oxer, if the back standards fall, I go to the front of the fence and put my measure so that the outside edge of the wing standard must come to the end of my measure. I have the measure set at the width I want the fence to be, on the front edge of the front wing standard. I do this because it is so much easier for me, rather than the people who are placing the wing standard, to be accurate.

In the case of a refusal, I may have to check the distance in a combination if it gets moved. In fact, I watch carefully all the time to see that fences are reset correctly. I also watch to see how all the fences jump, and two thirds of the way through the competition, I decide what exactly I am going to do for the jump-off, how many fences I will raise, and so on. I then go round to all my helpers and tell each pair exactly what I want done.

I always go and measure if I want the fence spread. In some cases raising the fence may mean adding an extra rail. Sometimes it is only necessary to raise the top rails. I always go round and check that all is correct and that the proper fences are crossed off. I find two very common faults are (a) to raise only the back rail of an ascending oxer, which turns it into a staircase fence, causing the distance in the combination to be different, and (b) if there are two rails above a wall, both will be raised, leaving too big a gap between the rails and the wall. This is

Fig. 15. A straight fence of solid-color planks in which all elements are placed vertically to the ground, one above the other.

Fig. 16. An Attractive Gate Type Fence. A good example of the variety that can be brought into a course if one has a good inventory of jump material.

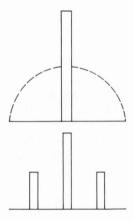

Fig. 17. Hog's Back Type of Fence

where I must decide whether to raise the top rail, or whether I can fit in an extra rail.

When the class is finished, I hope there is someone who can number the next course while I go round and reset the fences, heights, and spreads. If the Juniors and Amateurs are next, I suggest that 8C is only an upright fence, in which case the distance should be 25 feet 6 inches from 8B to 8C. I will hope for a higher proportion of clear rounds in Preliminary, Junior, and Amateur classes than in the Open and Intermediate classes.

All this has been for a one-day show, but it would work equally well for the first day of a show. On subsequent days I try and vary the tracks, the combinations, and the way I use the material as much as possible. I try and build up the horses' and riders' confidence, so that on the last day I can build a big course for the Grand Prix or other major competition, and hope to get six to eight clear rounds leading to a really exciting jump-off. In an important class I will raise and spread most of the fences for the jump-off, as it should be won primarily by jumping rather than by going fast.

Indoor Shows

For indoor shows the plans must be very much more accurate. I mark the sides of the arena in 10-foot lengths, starting from the center outward. On the plan I put all the distances in feet, and I mark the plan to correspond to the marks on the sides of the arena. As at an outdoor show, I try and use approximately the same track, but vary the route on the one day. It is not practical to lay out rails indoors, since these will be in the way of the tractor bringing in the material, but I generally put colored tape on the sides of the arena, so that other people can get on with building the outside fences, and I can concentrate on placing those in the center of the arena. Then, when the course is up, I can go round and check that the whole course is correct.

If the course plan is accurate, it should be easy to put the course in, but if one fence is incorrectly placed, then nothing will fit in. Indoors, the distances between fences are much less, thus it is more important for the course designer to pay attention to distances. Outside, the rider can very often decide to add or omit a stride to suit his horse, but this is much more difficult indoors. The basic distances, if the going is good, are 48 feet for three strides, 60 feet for four strides, and 72 feet for five strides.

The course designer must also take into consideration the type of

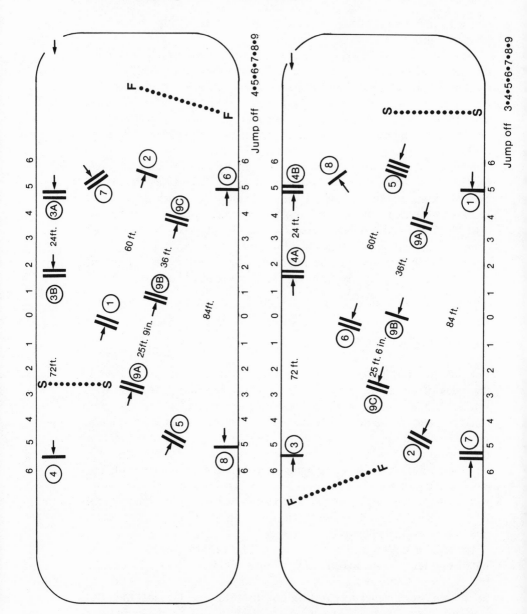

Fig. 18.   The course plans illustrate how the same indoor course plan can be used for two different competitions with the fences jumped in a different order and in different ways. They also show how distances must be worked out in greater detail than in outside courses, where the fences are not placed so close to each other.

fence he is using. An upright fence to a triple bar, going away from home, would be very long, just as a triple bar followed by an upright going toward home would be very short using these distances.

Course plans for an indoor arena should be simple. It is surprising the amount of variety that can be produced by varying the start and the finish and the type of fences used.

Working in a small arena, it is a great help if the width of the wing standards is reduced. This was done in New York and made my work much easier. It also gave the arena a much less crowded appearance. A few narrow fences can also be used. If the regular rails are 12 feet, the short ones should be 6 feet, as much of the filler material will be built in two halves and thus half a wall can be used. If a fence is narrow, it must be solid.

If a fence has to be jumped twice in a round, it must be quick to re-build. If it is jumped both ways it must be either an upright or a hog's back type, except in special competitions like a Gambler Stake when you must use oxers. The only answer to building an oxer to be jumped from both directions is that it must not have much filling, as this makes it dangerous, and the safety factor is all-important. I virtually never use an oxer jumped both ways, except in the special competitions, as it is so difficult to build a nice-looking oxer that is safe from both directions, whereas a straight or staircase type of fence can be combined so that it will appear different from the other direction. Again, if a fence is jumped twice in a round, it should never be used twice in the jump-off.

Permanent Fences

Permanent fences do make a course more interesting both for the spectators and the competitors, and I find that an arena with permanent fences, which have to be incorporated in the course for some competitions and avoided for others, is more interesting to plan for. Any strange fence should be used in the easiest possible way to begin with. Anything new tends to worry the riders, and to my way of thinking it is all-important to get the riders' and the horses' confidence.

Strangely enough, a dry ditch generally causes more trouble than a water ditch. I very much like to have a water ditch, as I think this is invaluable for getting young horses accustomed to a water jump. The ordinary water jump is never a problem to the horse if he arrives at the right point of takeoff. The horse's arc over a normal spread fence is frequently over 12 feet, but often the rider gets worried in his approach and loses his judgment of distance. The horse gets worried too and lands in the water, and so both horse and rider lose confidence.

For schooling young horses, I like to use a water ditch with a sloping brush in front and a rail over the middle, so that to begin with the horse doesn't realize the water is there. Later, you leave the rail off and gradually pull the brush back. Then take the brush away and go back to the rails over the middle and finally jump it as an oxer. When the horses are jumping this confidently, the rider should go to an ordinary water jump with brush and a rail over the water at about 2 feet 6 inches' height, slightly nearer to the brush than the landing edge. He should try and use it toward home, and if horses have been given confidence in this way, ninety-nine out of a hundred will have no trouble over water.

I always like to use a broad white lathe on the landing side of a water jump, even when I use a rail over, as I think in this way the horse learns that he must jump over the water. I like a water jump to be able to be jumped in both directions. In a flat arena this is possible, but it is always more difficult to jump water uphill, so this should be avoided. I don't like the water jump to be one of the major causes of faults in a competition. Great care must be taken in siting the fence before and after the water. Remembering the variation in length of a horse's stride, room must be given to the rider to adjust so that he arrives at the right point of takeoff. And the same applies to the fence after the water. I prefer to use at least a quarter or half turn to give the rider the opportunity to get his horse in hand before the fence, as is illustrated in my American Invitational Course (see Figure 19). At the same time, it is perfectly fair to put the next fence in line with the water, and I do use this.

One other factor I am always careful about with the water jump is that if I use it in a jump-off, I will never give a sharp turn into it, for in a class where speed has an influence the riders must chance turning in short and then the horse may land in the water and thereafter get careless. For the same reason I don't use a sharp turn after the water. Water jumps and ditches should always have a mat on the landing side to prevent a horse slipping if he lands in the water.

Ditches, wet and dry, can be used in many ways, and are a good test of a horse's courage. A dry ditch should never be more than 18 inches deep, as it is the hole in the ground that makes the horse look. He hasn't time to see how deep it is, and again, remember the safety factor.

Banks and ramps also give variation. The drop from the top of these must not be too high, and the surface must be solid and remain so for all the time it is in use. In my opinion, whereas water and all kinds of ditches are good to use in all general and Grand Prix competitions, I consider a bank is more an obstacle for a speed class or derby.

Big Shows

There is probably more choice of material for the big shows. Therefore, when working out the course plans, it is possible to put in fences
that are not used in every competition. I always try and use as much of
the heavy material, such as walls and pillars, on the first day, as there is
much less trouble moving it around in the arena than having to fetch it
from outside later in the show.

One can hope that a big show will have an arena at least 130 yards by
90 yards, as this gives so much more scope for interesting courses. If
there are permanent fences, use them in the easiest possible way. I generally don't use them for novice horses on the first day, but after that it
is a good idea to use them where possible, always remembering that
you want to use the ditch and water on the last day in the big competition, so if it is very wet you may have to substitute a fence at the side
to preserve the going for the final day. The plans must also be worked
out so that different ground is used each day.

A really big competition that is held in a stadium and is the only one
is possibly the most difficult course to design. The advantages are that
there is probably plenty of time to spend on dressing the fences and no
spoiled ground to avoid. Against this are the following problems:
How is the ground going to jump? How will the horses react to coming into a big stadium and jumping big fences without any warm-up
competitions?

As a show of several days progresses, I consider I get the feel of the
horses' capabilities and how the ground is going to jump. When I designed the course for the American Invitational in Tampa in 1973, I
knew how the horses had been jumping on the Florida circuit, but I still
had the two imponderables mentioned above to cope with. In this case
I put the course up on Tuesday, and then had to work at the Tampa
show on a very different ground all the rest of the week. People kept
asking me how many clear rounds I expected. With hope, but without
much confidence, I said between six and eight. I kept thinking that when
I got back to the ground I was going to alter this and that. But when I
returned there on Sunday morning, the course had been decorated in my
absence, and I got the feeling that it looked about right, and if I started
changing things I might unbalance the course.

Fences 1, 2, and 3 at 4 feet 6 inches, 4 feet 9 inches, and 4 feet 9
inches were fairly easy and got the horses going. Fences 4A and 4B, a
double of uprights after two spread fences and going toward home, were

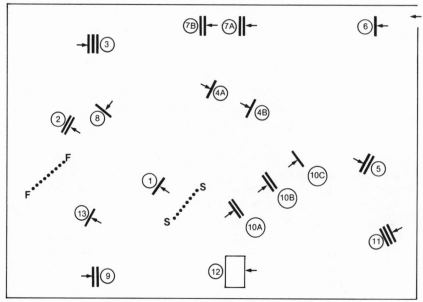

Jump off 3 • 4 • 5 • 6 • 7 • 8 • 9

Fig. 19.   American Invitational 1973

the first problem. These were 4 feet 9 inches and 5 feet high with 26 feet between, slightly short for big, impressive fences. Fence 5 was a square oxer 4 feet 9 inches and 5 feet 6 inches wide. This fence looked very white until we stapled some greenery onto the gate, which made all the difference to it. This was followed by a turn left-handed, and just past the entrance there was a straight wall at 5 feet 6 inches. From here the double of rustic oxers was 32 yards away, a good distance, but many people pitched over the wall, as it was big and was away from home. If this happened, the experienced riders realized they had to take back and put in an extra stride to be in a good position to jump the double, fence 7A, 4 feet 6 inches and 4 feet 9 inches high, and 6 feet wide over a 6-foot water ditch. Twenty-four feet to another oxer 4 feet 9 inches and 5 feet high, and 6 feet wide. If the less experienced riders pitched over the wall, they still tried to get to fence 7A and 7B in seven strides, so they arrived with the horse stretched out, and he hit the front rail of 7A or 7B or both.

Fence 8, a trough and rails at 5 feet, did not cause much bother, nor did 9, an oxer 4 feet 9 inches, 5 feet, and 5 feet 6 inches wide. The combination oxer to oxer measured 35 feet 6 inches from 10A (4 feet 6 inches, 4 feet 9 inches and 5 feet 3 inches wide) to 10B (4 feet 9 inches, 4 feet 9 inches, and 5 feet 6 inches wide) and 26 feet to 10C, an upright at 5 feet 3 inches. This jumped very well, and I did feel I could have put 10C at 5 feet 6 inches. At the same time the final result was eight prizes and eight clear rounds, so probably it was enough for early in the showing season.

Eleven was a triple bar 5 feet high and 6 feet wide, purposely an easy fence before the water. The water was really well constructed, the earth that was removed being built into banks at either side. This was 14 feet 6 inches wide and did cause a certain amount of trouble, mostly because riders got overanxious, for in the classes for amateurs and juniors that followed, with the triple bar and the water exactly the same, I think only two people faulted at it.

Fence number 13 consisted of upright rails at 5 feet 3 inches, and there were quite a few faults here. Just before the end, a very anxious Gene Mische, the show manager, came and said he hoped I'd get the eighth clear, as there were only eight ribbons and numerous horses with four faults. Much to his and my relief, the last horse went clear. This was a class that I was happy with. Other than the eight clears, there were very few with more than twelve faults. In the jump-off two horses went clear.

A really big competition should be won by jumping ability. Many people feel that a big competition should either have two rounds and a jump-off or one round and two jump-offs. But nowadays, when there are so many big competitions, I am inclined to feel you can obtain the same result without asking the horse to jump so many fences, provided the jump-off course is raised and widened sufficiently, with one round and one jump-off.

I have written much more fully of the ordinary shows, as it is here that the course designer is going to learn his job and needs guidelines. Gradually, as he starts working at bigger shows, he is going to develop his own method of obtaining results. Naturally he is going to make mistakes along the line, but providing he is prepared to admit these, and even apologize to the competitors for them, he is going to learn what he should not do.

We all have different theories about many things, for example, where to place a fence before the water jump. Some people consider that a fence at 49 feet 6 inches (15 meters) in front of the water helps a horse to jump the water. I think it helps the horse with the stride that fits into this distance, that is, the average stride, but for the long or short striding horse, it provides problems. Equally, the going may affect the distance, so I like to play safe and give the rider more opportunity to adjust his stride. But this is only my opinion.

At outdoor shows I like to have plenty of room between the fences, as I feel indoors there is so much jumping over closely related fences that it is a mistake to use these fences too often out of doors. I consider that it is less tiring for a horse to jump a course of twelve numbered fences, say, fifteen efforts, over a course of 650 yards than the same number of fences over 500 yards. But again, these are only my opinions. Certainly for novice horses, the longer distances between fences give the horses time to recover from mistakes. In the same way, in a Preliminary class for really green horses, I will not ask them to jump a treble combination until I know the horses have confidence over doubles. If they make a mistake, they can get into such terrible trouble at the last fence of a three combination.

I hope no one is going to get into trouble if they follow my guidelines at the start of their careers. I am sure there is much that I have omitted, but there is nothing like practical work for gaining experience. There is one thing I would emphasize. Take time to do the preparation properly. There are the few exceptional people who can walk into an arena and put up a course from a very rough sketch, but even these course designers will give the ring crew extra work; I defy anybody to regularly put up good courses from rough sketches without having to move fences once they are built. All my life I have benefited from having done my homework and thus have been able to concentrate all my thoughts on working from a prepared plan. I therefore have some chance of getting a good course built in the shortest possible time. I will never leave things that are not quite right without correcting them, as a good "jumpable" course is more important than a little extra time spent.

To sum up, the courses for novice horses and riders are all-important, for if they are well thought out they will help to produce horses and riders of the future. But it is the big competitions that are the ultimate test for the course designer, because if he can produce a really good public spectacle, this is what is going to make show jumping a really popular spectator sport.

Equitation Courses

GEORGE H. MORRIS

George H. Morris. A resident of Pittstown, New Jersey, and a graduate of the University of Virginia, George Morris began riding at the age of nine at the Ox Ridge Hunt Club in Darien, Connecticut, under Miss V. Felicia Townsend and Otto Heuckeroth. Later, he was a pupil of Gordon Wright. At the age of fourteen he won both the AHSA Medal and ASPCA Maclay finals, the youngest rider to ever do so.

Mr. Morris became a member of the United States Equestrian Team jumping squad in 1957. He rode on the team that won the gold medal at the Pan American Games in Chicago in 1959 and on the team that won the silver medal at the Olympic Games in Rome in 1960. At the latter he was placed fourth individually. Since becoming a professional trainer and instructor in 1964, he has trained champions in numerous hunter and jumper divisions at major American shows, and he has instructed sixteen of the national finalist winners in Medal and Maclay competition, in addition to riding many hunters and jumpers to championships himself.

Author of *Hunter Seat Equitation,* acknowledged as a definitive work in the field, he has also written articles for *Practical Horseman, Horse and Rider,* and the *Chronicle of the Horse.* In 1973 he was elected the American Horse Shows Association's "Horseman of the Year."

The course diagrams in this section were drawn by Jan Royce Conant.

What Is Hunter Seat Equitation?

By definition the name "hunter seat equitation" implies the riding of a horse for fox hunting purposes. But in terms of show ring terminology, this seat is used for a number of competitions and purposes from open jumping to bridle path hack classes. Some confusion has arisen in recent years with the increased interest that has developed in dressage, so that many people talk about the hunter seat versus the jumper seat versus the dressage seat. The term "hunter seat," however, was the one first used in connection with equitation over fences competition, and it is as good a term as any to describe the position that best enables the rider to ride a horse over fences and across country.

In comparing the look of a hunter seat to that of the other equitation seats, that is, saddle seat or stock seat, one must understand the rider's position on the horse in relation to what the horse is going to do. Theoretically our hunter seat rider is going to have to ride across country for long distances over uneven terrain. He is going to have to walk, trot, canter, gallop, and jump. He has to be flexible to keep up with the horse who is undertaking these various movements. The word that best defines the hunter seat rider is "workmanlike," one who appears to be in a position to cope with any problem that arises.

Because hunter seat riding is workmanlike riding on a horse able to perform a number of functions, the tack used on the horse and the clothing of the rider should also be functional and traditional. Anything artificial that does not relate to the job being done is wrong and unnecessary. The picture the judge is looking for is that of a well-tailored, clean, and neat rider, on a well-groomed horse, with a minimum of tack, in a balanced position on the horse, creating as little burden for the horse as possible both on the flat and over fences. The rider should have his weight well down in the stirrups with the heel down. The thighs and seat must give the impression of a glued connection with the horse during all sitting work and a lightness while posting, galloping, and jumping. The upper body must show tremendous flexibility and be in harmony with the motion of the horse at each gait and while taking a jump. The rider should be so attuned to the horse that he is able to ride in a forward, galloping position toward a jump and yet be able to sit down instantly, when necessary, and drive his horse with his back. As far as arms and hands are concerned, elasticity, following the horse's head and neck motion, and softness or sympathy are the best trademarks of the good rider. Sloppiness, stiffness, roughness, or passivity are all bad riding characteristics, detrimental to the horse's performance, and are not what is expected in the first-class hunter seat rider.

The Purpose of Hunter Seat Equitation

Now that we have defined the basics of a hunter seat, what is the purpose of this division as far as horse showing is concerned? My answer is that it is a training division — no more, no less. We are developing better riders by including this division in the curriculum at horse shows. Certainly one's riding ability should never be an end unto itself; it is rather a means toward the end, which is helping the horse perform better, be it across country or in Madison Square Garden. By having hunter seat equitation as a division at a show, the rider has many, many opportunities to practice riding and performing both on the flat and over fences. He becomes accustomed to various modified courses, which later on he will be asked to execute to show his horse off as a hunter or a jumper. And last, but by no means least, it gives the rider who cannot afford a top horse for hunter or jumper competition a chance to compete on equal footing with those financially more fortunate.

There are two categories of horse show competition for the equitation rider, one being on the flat (walk, trot, canter, and gallop) and the other over jumps. Although this book is about jumping courses, let me say that the foundation for jumping courses well lies in the preparation and is determined to a great extent by how well a rider can ride a horse on the flat. That is why so many hunter seat classes are judged either solely or at least partially at the walk, trot, and canter. The whole structure of a rider's jumping technique is built on the flat: security in the saddle, independence of different parts of the body, use of the aids, smoothness, coordination, and good habits are all made automatic through slow drill work on the flat. What a judge is looking for in a flat class is a good riding system built upon polished control.

Equitation over fences at various levels according to degree of skill or age of the rider serves the same purpose. It demonstrates basic position and control over a suitable course of jumps, giving the judge a chance to evaluate each rider's good and bad qualities. Is he a tight, secure rider or a bit loose? Is he an overrider (too strong) or an underrider (too weak)? Does he possess the basic understanding of a good riding system or is he talented but riding by the seat of his pants? Does he have a good eye for a distance or a poor sense of timing? Is he soft and sympathetic with his horse or a bit of a butcher? These are just some of the things that cross a judge's mind as he watches twenty, forty, or·sixty riders compete (or even one hundred and eighty in the Medal finals). He must evaluate and compare over and over again until he comes up with the answer as to who is the best rider.

I find that equitation over fences classes prepare and develop the hunter and jumper riders of tomorrow and, I feel, should be looked upon as that and not more. Otherwise the point of equitation classes is apt to be lost and American riding would suffer a good deal. Don't forget that the quest for a blue ribbon only can be a very dangerous thing!

Training over Jumps

The number, types, and series of obstacles used for training horse and rider are infinite. Modern show riding has become so sophisticated and complex that one must be familiar with almost every conceivable problem. It virtually takes years to graduate a beginner (Maiden) rider to a top-flight USET Equitation class winner at a major show. Not only must he negotiate the various courses of jumps, but he must do so smoothly and flawlessly, his aids being invisible, and his technique letter-perfect. In developing the rider to take these courses of fences, the instructor concentrates on one segment at a time rather than many jumps in a series at once. When each little part is broken down, understood, and then mastered, it makes taking the whole so much easier. While most individual fences used for practice are also used within the courses in competition, there are a few obstacles used for training only — namely, the cavaletti, crossed-rail fence, and the no-stride in-and-out.

Let's start with the cavaletti. A cavaletti is a rail or a series of rails (no more than three or four) lying on the ground or a few inches above the ground. The horse is to step over these rails but never to jump them. Their purpose is to introduce a horse to an obstacle quietly. By stepping and not jumping the horse is much more apt to stay calm and to learn not to associate a barrier in his path with rushing forward. At the same time the rider is acquiring the habit and feel of regulating the horse's pace rather than vice versa. Most cavaletti work is done at the trot, usually posting, but occasionally, at a more advanced stage, sitting. It is amazing how well a rider can establish so many of his basics stepping over a rail without even taking a jump — his upper body inclined with the motion of the horse, eye control, leg position, riding a line, release of his hold on the horse's mouth, and control of his horse. All this homework makes the first actual jump very, very easy.

Probably more horses and riders have left the ground first over a crossed-rail fence than over any other jump — and for good reason. A crossed-rail fence (or an *X*) is composed of two rails, one end of which is up off the ground about 1 foot and the other resting on the ground. This makes the jump about 6 inches in the center, a very low jump and one that encourages horse and rider from the start to automatically seek the middle of the fence, something terribly important later on in riding courses. Again, due to the simplicity of the crossed-rail fence, we can work on our rider's basics, which we worked on over the cavaletti. Of course now we are experiencing the horse's flight in the air for the first time, and this necessitates holding our hands and arms forward over the jump and also keeping our upper body forward. One must be sure not to drop back over the fence with either the upper body or hands, or to look down to the ground, or to lose the vital security of the lower leg position on the side of the horse.

The straight-rail or vertical jump is next. The only difference between this fence and the crossed-rail is that the height of the jump remains the same the length of the fence, which forces the rider to hold his horse straight. Also a straight-rail is usually the next step in height after the crossed-rail, which really gives the rider the feeling of a bigger jump — not just a little hop.

There are essentially only two kinds of fences to jump: a straight up-and-down fence (vertical) and a wide-jump (spread). With the exception of open ditches and water, which are rarely, if ever, used in hunter seat equitation classes, all spreads are composed of height and width. Width creates a new dimension for the rider, that of jumping across a fence. While this new feeling is very easy for the more advanced rider to cope with, it is definitely a problem for the beginner — psychologically as well as physically — and therefore should be faced at an early stage. I like to start my beginners over very small spreads soon after they have graduated from the crossed-rail to the straight-rail. Of course the danger of spread fences is that the rider tends to come back too early in the air with his body, his hands, or both. Resting and pressing on the horse's crest with both hands is a good exercise to counteract this fault, and concentrating on holding the hip angle closed far forward after landing will take care of the upper body habit.

When introducing spread fences, I like to do it in a sequence of increasing difficulty: First, the step oxer, where a lower element is backed up by a higher one; second, the hog's back, a higher element in the center with a lower one in front and behind; third, the triple bar, a little harder in that it is a succession of rails graduating upward from front to back, often causing the horse to jump long and flat; then the most difficult spread fence, the square oxer, which is the same height in front as it is in back, creating two problems at once, the vertical and the spread.

Once the rider has been started nicely over these single low obstacles, it is time to move on to combinations of fences. A combination is any series of two or more fences within 39 feet 4 inches of each other. When 40 feet separate two jumps, it is no longer considered a combination or in-and-out but rather two separate jumps. When dealing with combinations so close together, it is imperative that the riding teacher be thoroughly familiar with striding. Otherwise, bad accidents will occur as a result of conflicts with the horse's stride. Remember that a horse working at a canter (14 to 16 miles per hour) has, on average, a 12-foot stride. Don't forget the variables, though. Is it a big horse, a little horse, or a pony? What kind of a stride does he have? Is there a good footing or heavy mud? Is the mount a green horse that hangs back or a bold horse that rushes his jumps? The average sixteen-hand horse working with a 12-foot stride lands about 6 feet after and takes off about 6 feet in front of a fence. Therefore we arrive at multiples of 12 feet when working with combinations and distances between single fences. Here are some of the standard combination spacings.

No-stride in-and-out fences are usually 12 feet apart, sometimes a foot or two less. Often this type of combination is called a "bounce" and is a good exercise for teaching a rider to hold his position and balance. Because of its tightness this combination is kept quite low, as a rule, and hardly, if ever, used as part of a course in competition. It is strictly a schooling exercise.

The one-stride in-and-out, on the other hand, is common to almost all courses. The distance between the fences can range greatly, from a very short 16 feet to a very long 30 feet, with 24 feet being a norm. Showing distances for one-stride combinations in hunter classes are fixed of course by rules according to the size and greenness of horse or pony, although in equitation it is left up to the course builder. As an exercise at home I start the rider thinking of lengthening or shortening his horse with the one-stride combination. This provides him with an opportunity to practice and coordinate the use of his aids: hands, legs, weight, voice, stick, and spurs. This ability to lengthen and shorten is really what jumping fences, series of fences, and courses are all about. It is what we call measuring or placing the horse to the fence and is known as timing.

The two-stride combination is much the same as the one-stride except there is more time for the rider to adjust the striding, the average distance between the two fences being about 36 feet. One can do a very short two at 30 feet or a very long two at 42 feet, providing the horse is flexible and athletic. Again, the riding exercises employed in the one-stride in-and-out can be repeated and reviewed in the two-stride in-and-out. A good practice exercise through these close quartered jumps is to ask a rider either to hold his galloping (two-point) position between the fences or to drop down into his saddle (three-point) from one jump to another. This will enable a rider to either underride an in-and-out smoothly or override strongly, both approaches being useful to the more advanced technician.

Lines of fences, while not as close as combinations, can still be ridden more accurately up to ten strides apart by knowing whether the number of strides should be short, medium, or long. Take for example two fences set 60 feet apart. By landing 6 feet away from fence 1 and galloping slowly four strides (12 feet per stride) one would arrive 6 feet away from the next fence, a perfect distance. Now if the rider arrived at the first fence a bit short, he would have to regain his momentum and move on to arrive at the perfect place for fence 2. Or, conversely, if he jumped the first fence too boldly, he would have to shorten his horse's stride to have a good second fence. While this does make timing a bit mechanical, as I have said, it does gain precision in show riding, and that is a terribly important part of a good performance. Just remember the number of strides between jumps is not nearly so important as knowing whether to shorten or lengthen the horse's stride to get the correct number.

What a course of jumps really boils down to is jumping fences on lines and off turns. Therefore one must consider and practice turns in conjunction with lines from the very start. The single most important factor in working with jump-off turns is whether or not the rider is using his eyes correctly. Not only is the turn and the line to the fence determined by the rider's eyes but so too is judging the correct takeoff for the fence. The rider must practice, in order to sharpen up his eye, jumping off long, sweeping turns and also off short, abrupt turns. Both are good exercises. Holding the horse between hands, legs, and seat on the track or line of the turn is of utmost importance. Not allowing the horse to bulge out or to cut in on the turn and maintaining the horse's balance and pull on the turn are all points to be practiced and repracticed. Smooth turns in equitation classes often separate good rounds with more or less even performance over the fences. In dealing with turns as a teacher, I am very concerned with the rider straightening up his body a bit and sinking a little deeper into the saddle on the turn in order to help balance his horse back on his hocks. This is where upper body control directly aids in controlling the horse.

Jumping fences at an angle is really not for the beginner; too much control with the rider's hands is required during the late approach, during takeoff, and even in flight to ask a rider in a low grade to attempt this. Jumping fences on an angle requires what we call jumping out of hand, which is keeping a direct feel of a horse's mouth while taking a jump. The rider with insufficient security, balance, or timing will invariably get left behind and will pull on his horse's mouth. This will produce a horse that stops or runs out at fences. For this reason I do not encourage the teaching of angling jumps until I am sure of a rider's ability. The first fence of a combination is particularly risky to angle much at all. Unless a horse and rider are terribly coordinated, a run-out at the second fence is likely to occur.

Most courses in the hunter seat equitation division are set up within an oval or rectangular arena, with two long sides and two short sides. Therefore, one is accustomed to setting practice fences on a line up the long side, on the end, or perhaps down the diagonal of the ring from one corner to the opposite corner. These are the most popular positions to put fences. Of course there are a thousand variations to this pattern: from the long side down the diagonal and vice versa; down the center of the ring; across the middle of the ring; a figure-eight pattern using two diagonals; a figure eight through the center using the long sides; a serpentine down the center of the ring. And to keep my riders sharp, at home I constantly vary the way I set the jumps, working with these common patterns yet always changing them around a bit. One of the more unusual lines I call a circular line, which follows the track of a semicircle, using three jumps, one at the beginning, middle, and end of the curve.

An outside course is another good test of horsemanship; but while shows are encouraged to hold a class in the equitation division over such a course, they rarely do, mainly because the hunters are so busy in that area. An outside course is a wonderful teaching exercise in setting a pace, holding it, and measuring the jumps as they come along out of this pace. For some riders this even pace, where the horse carries them along, makes their timing better, and for others it makes it worse. Regardless, it is a great way to get the feel of a more open gallop between the fences and is good for a rider's eye for distance. This kind of course should be inviting in that the fences are several panels wide, solid-looking, and with good ground lines to help the galloping horse set himself. The fences should be placed far enough apart and on nice sweeping lines, so that one can show a flowing pace.

To sum up, I will school at home over a ring course as a whole. While I am more apt to school over cavaletti, combinations, single fences, or segments of courses from day to day, I will, especially before a big show such as Devon, or the big Eastern indoor fall circuit, use a full, complete course in my teaching. I am most careful on my courses to keep them full of variety. I want several changes of direction, a line with a long distance, a line with a short distance, fences on a turn, a double and a treble combination, and often a single fence sitting in the middle of the ring that can often "get" a rider from its very simplicity. While working over this course I try to correct the picture of the rider as a whole. Observing the rider from afar taking a complete course, one sees all the little things to work on the next day when going back to the cavaletti or the single fence. Riding the complete course is a good exercise in itself, but it is much too long and generalized for working out basic faults in technique.

Showing over Courses

Now I am going to explain what the categories of the riders are, what is expected of riders at particular levels, and what kind of course they should be up to jumping. The American Horse Shows Association (AHSA), the national equestrian federation of the United States, has very ably over the years put together the equitation division level by level, allowing the equitation rider to progress in steps. He is thus able to compete with riders of his own grade and age and is not forced to go out of his category until he proves by winning blue ribbons that he is ready. It is a very nice system, as it provides plenty of easy classes for riders starting out on their showing careers, assuring them of lots of practice. Only through repetition is one's technique made sound and do the butterflies subside, paving the way for advanced riding over harder courses.

The jumping class that most show ring riders first enter is Maiden over Fences. A Maiden rider is one who has never won an equitation class over fences at a recognized AHSA horse show. Winning on the flat does not affect a Maiden rider's status over fences. While he can advance on the flat and not affect his status, the reverse is not true. Once a rider has eliminated himself from an equitation category over fences, he is no longer eligible for that same category in the flat. The reasoning behind this rule is that anyone who is able to win over jumps has really done the hard part and should not compete doing the easier work at walk, trot, and canter. It seems to work well this way and to be fair to all.

What we are looking for in judging a Maiden rider is not someone who is able to jump high and wide and show advanced controls, but rather one who has the basics of a good position, use of aids, and simple controls. The four basic parts of the rider's body upon entering the ring should be controlled and well placed: the stirrup on the ball of the foot, the heel down and in behind the girth, and the calf in light contact with the horse; the thighs and seat firm, the posting trot clear, the sitting trot deep; the transition from canter to gallop clearly marked by a change from two- to three-point contact; the upper body flexible in that the hip angle shows approximately the right angulation forward for each gait; the eyes up and ahead in anticipation of any turns. While judging a Maiden rider, I want to see basic controls of holding a pace around a course and riding fairly accurate lines to the jumps with as little cutting in or bulging out as possible. The release should be either to the mane or crest, not "out of hand," as the rider's security and timing are not up to that yet. On the turns he should balance his horse, slightly steadying his pace and displacing his weight down into his horse a bit by straightening up his body and sinking into the saddle. All his controls should be definite yet smooth; and while even at this stage a rider must "get" his eight fences to win at a big show, his eye for distance must be natural and apparent, yet need not be dead accurate. In other words, a Maiden rider must show the stamp of a correct foundation. He is not going to be polished and perfect; he often will not be dressed as a grownup (jodhpurs instead of boots and breeches); he will look quite good if things go well but will not be able to cover up if things go wrong; his riding will be obvious, not always invisible and subtle. And because the depth of his security, position, and control over jumps is so shallow, we do not want to add insult to injury by asking him to jump anything but the simplest course.

In recent years the AHSA divisional committees have become more and more specific in setting requirements for different classes. The Equitation Hunter Seat Committee felt that an exact guideline was required for course designers and management of each category of this division, as far as courses were concerned. In all classes the course must be held over at least six obstacles. This is to give the judge enough time to eval-

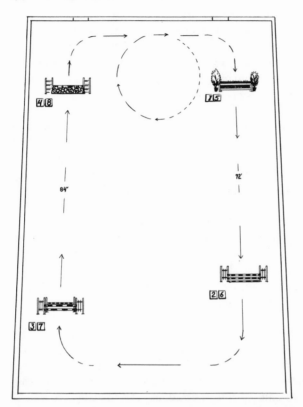

Fig. 1.   Course for Maiden Equitation (no fence to exceed 3′ and wings to be of at least 30″). (1, 5) brush, 2′6″; (2, 6) rails, 2′9″; (3, 7) rail oxer, 2′0″ and 3′0″ x 2′0″; (4, 8) coop, 3′0″.

uate each performance. In Maiden classes over fences, no jump may exceed 3 feet, and wings of at least 30 inches in width must be used, insuring a relatively low course in height, and providing a preventive measure against run-outs. A Maiden course is not required to have combinations or a change of direction, which really means that these added difficulties should not be part of the test; it should be kept simple. In fact my idea of a fine Maiden course (see Figure 1) is twice around the ring over four jumps, each taken twice. This gives the judge ample time and opportunity to study each rider and his performance, and yet the course is not too long or difficult for anyone. I feel any conventional small hunter-jumper type fence will do (see Figures 2, 3, and 4). If a spread is used I would keep it quite narrow (2 feet); and if a colorful jump is part of the course I would not want it to be too spooky. The

Figs. 2, 3, and 4.   Obstacles. Figures 2 and 3 are examples of good obstacles for Maiden and Novice courses. They are solid and inviting. Figure 4 is an example of an airy fence that could be made acceptable by the addition of another rail between the stone wall and the top rail. Note that the empty cups have not been removed, which is bad as they can be dangerous in a fall if the rider hits the wing of the fence. Every effort should be made to have the fences of Maiden and Novice courses as varied as those for the most advanced classes, making full use of filler material and the blocks for raising the height of a wall, as shown in these fences. (Photos by Budd.)

jumps should be very jumpable and inviting to the horse. The ground lines should be clear and there should be no airy jumps. Also, the distance from the center of one fence on a line to the next should be measured, and multiples of 12 feet used (the number of multiples according to the size of the ring). There is no need to impose difficulties as far as striding goes, either for Maidens or for Novices, the next category of ability. As soon as the course builder varies from the exact multiples of twelve, he or she is asking horse and rider to shorten or lengthen strides, and we are not ready for that in this category of performance.

The big difference between a Maiden and a Novice equitation rider is that the Maiden looks like a beginner and the Novice does not. A Novice is one who has not won three first-place ribbons in equitation over fences. Needless to say, one expects more of the Novice. His security is stronger just from the fact that his lower leg position is deeper and tighter and is not loosened as quickly by the unforeseen; his base of support looks a bit more glued to the horse — not jellylike; his upper body shifts with the motion of the different gaits more automatically; and one has the feeling by watching his eyes work that he is surer of himself than is a Maiden rider. Also, his hands and arms have taken on a smoother elasticity and do not tend to bounce around at the unexpected. A Novice's transitions from one gait to another and in holding a pace should be clearer and more precise, providing he is not overmounted on a horse that is too difficult. A crest release up the neck about a third of the way is what we are looking for, no longer any grabbing of the mane. His timing should be coming a bit into focus in that he meets his fences right a good deal of the time, not ahead or behind his horse. There is also often a difference in dress between the Maiden and the Novice toward the more mature appearance. Boots and breeches are worn rather than jodhpurs, and usually his clothes fit better. One can see that this level of rider, even though a neophyte, is becoming a show rider rather than a late entry.

The compulsory course requirements for Novice classes are identical to Maiden classes save for one factor. The one big difference is that there must be a change of direction in a Novice course. This is to demonstrate not only that the rider's basic position and control are equally good going both ways in the ring but that he is able to handle turns smoothly and in control. Also, he might be able to show a change of leg on the turns, which certainly would be a plus over one who could not. Actually from a judge's point of view it is interesting to note how few riders have positions that are equally good on their left and right sides, especially at these lower levels of competition. A good example of a

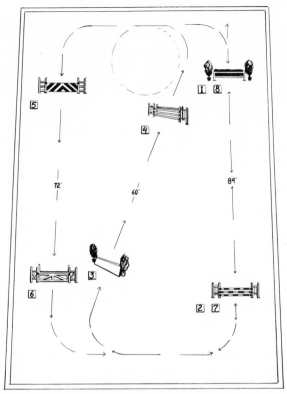

Fig. 5. Course for Novice Equitation (no fence to exceed 3′ in height and wings to be of at least 30″). (1, 8) brush, 3′0″; (2, 7) rails, 3′0″; (3) coop, 3′0″; (4) rail oxer, 3′0″ x 2′0″; (5) colored panel, 3′0″; (6) white gate and rail oxer, 2′9″ x 2′0″.

Novice course (Figure 5) would be up the side to the right, down the diagonal, and then once around the ring to the left. The course could be composed of eight jumps, several of which could be spreads, the distances all easy multiples of twelve. I feel it is very important to incorporate little, narrow spreads (2 to 3 feet) into these courses for psychological if for no other reason. Often beginners think that a spread is much more difficult to jump than a vertical, which, of course, it is not. Some color as far as the jumps are concerned could be a little more challenging, though nothing too spooky, please!

For a rider to graduate to the Limit classes over fences has always been quite an exciting hurdle to overcome. First, to win six blue ribbons over jumps is a goodly number; second, he has now become more or less an Open rider. He has graduated into high school, so to speak, and real polish and pressure are starting to become apparent. As a matter of fact, a top Limit rider can, occasionally, win the Open, Medal, or Maclay at the same show. He is that close to the big time! While the Limit's position is deeper, tighter, and more automatic than the Novice's, the big difference can really be seen in his strength and control. There is no question as to whether or not he is a passenger or a rider; he can cope with the unexpected quite well, covering up the difficulties to some degree. A competent technician is starting to emerge out of the child with potential. The good Limit boy or girl is really the about-to-be Open rider. Another characteristic of this riding level are hands that are not only smoother and more educated but now need to do almost nothing at takeoff in order to follow the mouth. As I have said, in the more elementary classes, because of lack of security and balance, I like to see the rider release his horse by resting his hands up his horse's crest about a third of the way. This is to insure enough freedom for the horse's head and neck and to take no chance of coming back on his mouth. But at the Limit level this exaggeration would really be too elementary, and there would be no need for it. An inconspicuous and natural release is what we want.

The course for Limit equitation still requires that no jump be over 3 feet and that wings of at least 30 inches in width be used. These simplicities fit the rider's level, and put a premium on basics such as position, use of aids, control, and smoothness rather than skills of a very sophisticated nature. It is most important for teachers, judges, and course designers alike to all remember that we are primarily interested in each phase of an equitation rider's progression, to emphasize and evaluate his correct foundation rather than to just look for a strong rider who has little else. Classic riding is what we are creating and that must be remembered always. One can see strong competitors all over the world, but there are relatively few equestrian artists compared to what we have in the United States.

Getting back to Limit courses, the one new requirement is that there must be a combination as well as a change of direction. One thus sees how gradually and sensibly each class category is made a bit more difficult, so as not to overface or discourage the young rider coming on. A good example of a Limit course (see Figure 6) would be up the side on the right hand, over a vertical and a small oxer, down the other side over a vertical and a combination of verticals, up the diagonal over an oxer and a vertical, turn left and finish backward over the first fence. Let me repeat again that I would strongly advise course designers to use multiples of twelve up through Limit and Under Fourteen classes. Do

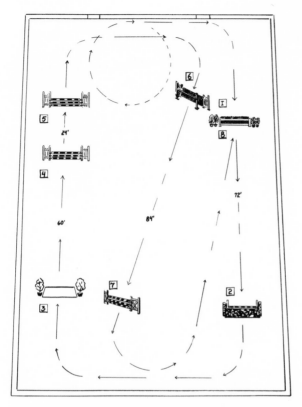

Fig. 6.   Course for Limit Equitation (no fence to exceed 3′ in height, wings to be of at least 30″). (1, 8) brush, 3′0″; (2) stone wall and rail oxer, 2′9″ and 3′0″ x 2′0″; (3) coop, 3′0″; (4) rails, 3′0″; (5) rails, 3′0″ (24′ combination); (6) colored panel, rail oxer, 3′0″ and 3′0″ x 2′0″; (7) planks, 3′0″.

not ask those below an Intermediate level to solve more complex distance problems. That is not what should be judged at these more elementary levels, and there is always the risk of an unnecessary fall in jumping a tricky distance.

Of all classes in the equitation division, I would say that those restricted to riders under fourteen bring together the most divergent riding levels and abilities. The variation can be enormous. Very often Maiden riders are competing against a precocious thirteen-year-old who at the same show is getting good Maclay-Medal ribbons. Therefore, you must be prepared for anything when you step in to judge this age group. My winner is apt to be one of the more polished riders of the whole show and my fourth-place competitor a nice Novice with potential! It is

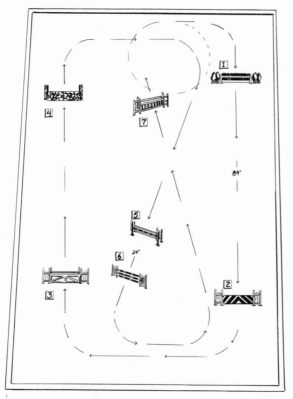

Fig. 7.   Course for Open Equitation under Fourteen (no fence to exceed 3′ in height, wings to be at least 30″). (1) brush, 3′0″; (2) painted panel, 3′0″; (3) white gate and rail oxer, 2′9″ and 3′0″ x 2′0″; (4) stone wall, 3′0″; (5) rail oxer, 2′6″ and 2′9″ x 3′0″; (6) rails, 3′0″ (24′ combination); (7) natural brown gate and rail oxer, 3′0″ and 3′0″ x 2′0″.

really hard to prescribe what standard to look for and expect, as this class usually fluctuates more than any other one.

Bearing this in mind, you must provide a course similar to our preceding Limit class: the jumps cannot exceed 3 feet; wings should be at least 30 inches wide; and one change of direction and a combination are required. As I have said, while there might be some very sophisticated under-fourteen-year-olds competing, the course must be kept simple for the norm of this age group. I'd be most satisfied to judge basic qualities of the riders over a course of four fences, once around the ring to the right, up the diagonal over a combination, and finishing down the alternate diagonal jumping a single fence (see Figure 7). As we shall see later, the single fence can be a problem unto itself, allowing horses and riders too much time to think, and thus rush into trouble.

The Intermediate classes are relatively new to the equitation division. They are open to those riders who have not won twelve blue ribbons over fences, and in a sense are almost of an Open class standard. The purpose of this category is to provide a few more classes for those who are out of Limit and yet are not really accomplished Maclay-Medal type riders. It gives them more classes and opportunity for practice and experience, and the psychology of having a few more blue ribbons under their belt is not bad either.

In evaluating an Intermediate rider, I am really looking at one who is just under the very small percentage of top Open horsemanship riders. His position is set; his aids work smoothly and invisibly; and his controls are strong, not only in his original round but also in executing any of the various AHSA tests allowed for this class. A good Intermediate is almost wholly polished, well dressed, and very aware of ring showmanship in general. There is nothing left between this stage and the final stage of top Open competition, save more experience and a big reputation. Do not forget, horse showing is like any other form of theatrical endeavor: a great deal depends upon one's public image and reputation for excellence. These are important ingredients that cannot be overlooked.

While the height for an Intermediate horsemanship course is only 3 feet 3 inches, it really should closely approach a regular Open equitation course in difficulty. There must be at least one change of direction and a combination, one fence of which must be a spread. I would strongly recommend incorporating some minor distance problems at this stage, requiring riders not only to control a pace in general, but also to show their ability to shorten and lengthen their horse's stride at will. A practical course (Figure 8) would be to enter the ring on a circle to the right, proceed up the diagonal of the ring over a vertical and an oxer 72 feet apart, make a left turn around the end of the ring, coming down the side over an oxer, turn left through the center over a vertical and then right over another spread fence. At this point make a right turn around the end of the ring, coming up the long side over a 25-foot in-and-out including a vertical and a spread, and going on to fence number 3, an oxer, going the other direction. The distances from the second part of the combination to this fence could be 48 feet. After going around the end of the ring again, turn right down the far side, finishing over a vertical and fence number 5, a triple bar, 82 feet apart. As you can see, I have varied slightly, in two places, from the exact multiples of twelve; and in so doing I am asking to see a bit more riding precision. Smooth

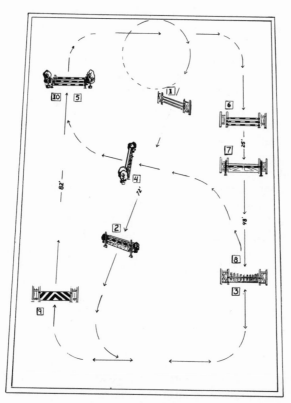

Fig. 8.   Course for Intermediate Equitation. (1) rails, 3′0″; (2) stone wall
and rail oxer, 3′0″ and 3′3″ x 3′0″; (3, 8) white gate and rail oxer, 2′9″
and 3′0″ x 2′0″; (4) stone wall, 3′0″; (5, 10) rail oxer, 2′6″ and 2′9″ x 3′0″;
(6) rails, 3′0″; (7) natural brown gate and rail oxer, 3′0″ and 3′0″ x 2′0″
(25′ combination); (9) striped panel, 3′0″.

precision in solving distance problems and turns is ultimately what we
want to see and that is what advanced riding is all about.

Basically, Open classes, Medal, Maclay, National Professional Horsemen's Association (PHA), and equitation championships are all the
same, the only difference being that the Medal and the Maclay competitions become easier to win as the year goes along because riders, as they
qualify, are no longer eligible to compete.

An established Open horsemanship rider, as a rule, is in a class of
excellence. His position is tight and he has a style of his own. There is
no question as to his use of aids, and they should by now be absolutely
automatic and invisible. The rider's positive strength and firmness of

control over his horse is now taken for granted, coupled with softness and sympathy in coping with the animal's limitations and shortcomings. All in all, an accomplished horseman is in evidence, and as often as not, he is a better craftsman in his technique than his age mates. At the better shows, riders at this level are turned out immaculately and so are their horses. The presentation of horse and rider gives the judge his first impression of the performance he is judging and is of the upmost importance. Any sort of sloppiness or dirtiness is really going to be a detriment. Not only must an Open rider be able to enter the ring and turn in a quality performance, but he must be able to perform all of the AHSA tests from which the judge may choose in making his final decision. Perhaps the most difficult test, the one which surely exposes the rider's good and bad points, is that of changing horses and rejumping part or all of the course. While a rider may be well able to deal with the familiar, his own horse, very often his lack of feel and experience causes him to fall apart on a strange animal. This is not uncommon; for this reason I like to give this test in important Open and Championship competitions. I expect a great deal of a good Open rider. After all, he has passed through many grades and is now in high school, ready to go on to college and graduate into the realm of a horse trainer or riding teacher.

As this is a book about courses for equitation classes rather than about equitation itself, I am going to outline three demonstration courses for this category of rider: one for Open and Championship classes; one for the Medal class; and one for the Maclay. Fences in these classes may be up to 3 feet 6 inches, and wings are optional.

An Open, National PHA, or a Championship course should ask a lot. The best riders at the horse show are likely to be in these classes, and possibly not in the Medal and Maclay, and they should be examined in a sophisticated fashion. Please do not misinterpret this to mean that a trap or artificial trick should be set. I detest the unnatural or the gimmicky above all things in dealing with horse and rider. Difficult questions asked in equestrian competition should only be compounded in a natural and possible direction, stretching the athletic scope rather than encouraging the freak. My sample course (Figure 9) for the class is as follows: The rider may either circle to the first fence on the right or left lead, as the first line will go up the center of the ring. The first fence will be a brush, followed in 48 feet by a step oxer, followed in 62 feet by a vertical, colored panel. This line requires a rider to be strong and aggressive right off the bat upon entering the ring. The distances require a long three strides followed by a long four strides, plus the fact that the horse is possibly going to drop back and spook at the panel. At the end

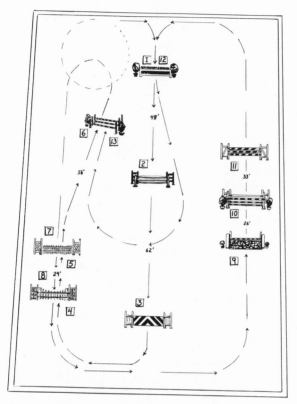

Fig. 9.   Course for Open, National PHA, or Championship Equitation. (1, 12) brush, 3'6"; (2) brown rail oxer, 3'0" and 3'6" x 3'0"; (3) panel, 3'6"; (4, 8) riviera gate, 3'6"; (5, 7) picket gate, 3'6"; (6, 13) rail triple bar, 2'6", 3'0", and 3'6"; (9) stone wall and rail oxer, 3'0", 3'6" x 3'0"; (10) rails, 3'6", 3'6", and 3'6" (26' combination); (11) planks, 3'6" (33' combination).

of the ring turn right over a vertical combination, with 24 feet between; then diagonally down the ring 56 feet to a triple bar. This part of the course necessitates getting one's horse together quickly, yet smoothly, taking a turn, and jumping down quite a tight line showing control. After the sixth fence (each part of a combination is counted as a separate fence in equitation and hunter classes), I want a left turn going back up the long side of the ring over the vertical combination in the other direction. This gives the rider a bit of a breather and also the opportunity of jumping a fence off a long approach, sometimes a problem in itself. After rounding the end of the ring to the left, we will jump a triple combination of a step oxer followed in 26 feet by a square oxer, followed in 33 feet by a vertical plank jump. This, also, is a distance variance and requires one long stride followed by two short ones. To finish this course, we will come back up the ring over fence 1, go around fence 2, and jump fence 6 again as a last fence. This last part shows great control in turning, which sometimes is more difficult toward the end of the ride when one's horse is a bit strong.

The course for an AHSA Hunter Seat Medal class must be a figure-eight course and contain two changes of direction rather than one. There must also be at least one combination. The reason behind the figure-eight course is that twenty-five years ago the Equitation Committee wanted to insure a more sophisticated course for this class, more than the usual twice around. Of course this is now outdated, as most equitation classes at good shows require turns, in-and-outs, and so on. The wording, however, has not been changed, and a good course designer is obligated to pay strict attention to the course following a figure-eight track. As long as there is one complete figure eight within the course, the rest of the course can go anywhere else it likes. In other words, one does not have to follow the figure-eight pattern the whole time, although I am going to illustrate a course in which two figure eights take up the whole. (Before going on, let me point out that I am laying out distances that could be used in an indoor ring of 100 feet by 200 feet. If the ring were bigger I would add strides on the lines, and if smaller I would subtract strides. Of course the combination strides would have to stay the same.)

To begin our Medal course (Figure 10), the rider enters the ring on a circle to the right and proceeds up the diagonal over an oxer followed 72 feet away by a vertical panel. He makes a left turn at the end of the ring and jumps a narrow garden gate; he turns left again down the opposite diagonal, jumping a vertical rail followed in 48 feet by rails and brush, then again followed in 58 feet by a stone wall. This makes up the first half of the course, which is a figure-eight pattern requiring the rider to start out over a spread and continue on for five nice strides to the next fence. He must then quickly yet smoothly collect his horse for the end fence, which, being narrow, could invite a run-out. After the next turn the rider must go forward three strides and immediately bring his horse back for a short four. The difficulty on this part of the course is really because the end fence does not give a rider much time to reorganize himself. Things happen in rapid succession and that is where the stumbling block is, not so much in the distances, fences, or turns. After completing the second diagonal, the rider follows the ring to the right and jumps an oxer close off the corner on the long side. It is often more difficult to jump spreads going away from the in gate and off tight turns

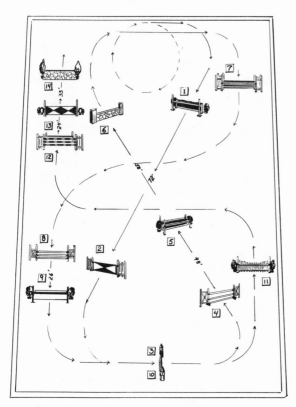

Fig. 10.   Course for AHSA Medal Class. (1) brush and rail, 3′3″ and 3′6″ x 3′0″; (2) panel, 3′6″; (3, 10) narrow garden gate, 3′3″; (4) rails, 3′6″; (5) rails and brush, 2′6″, 3′0″, and 3′6″ x 3′6″; (6) stone wall, 3′6″; (7) rail oxer, 3′0″ and 3′6″ x 3′0″; (8) rails, 3′6″; (9) coop and rail oxer, 3′3″ and 3′6″ x 3′6″ (26′ combination); (11) riviera gate, 3′6″; (12) rails, 3′3″ and 3′6″ x 3′6″; (13) panel, 3′6″ (24′ combination); (14) stone wall, 3′6″ (33′ combination).

due to the fact that impulsion is sometimes diminished at these spots. The rider then turns right through the middle of the ring, a left turn at the next long side, whereupon he jumps a long, 26-foot one-stride combination composed of a vertical and an oxer. He re-jumps the end fence, turns left down the long side over a gate, turns left again through the center of the ring to the opposite long side, and makes a right turn to a combination of an oxer, 24 feet, a vertical, 33 feet, and another vertical. This is the end of the course, and the apparent difficulty in this half of the course is in making all right-angle turns and jumping combinations out of them. I do like Medal courses to be a bit sophisticated, and I also like to use the figure-eight pattern throughout the course. As I have said, Medal courses have always been associated with this figure eight, and it is very easy to build courses using that kind of track, so why not!

When one builds a course for the Medal with an open jumper flavor, I like the Maclay to go in the direction of a hunter course. Do not forget, equitation is a preparation and practice division, making well-rounded horsemen for tomorrow. We want riders equally at home on both hunters and jumpers. Now I am not saying that the Medal course should be built for the jumper and the Maclay course for the hunter, but I do like this different emphasis when both classes are offered.

In setting my Maclay class for this hypothetical horse show, I am going to think of getting a hunter performance out of the riders. They should be able to set a pace and flow around this course with imperceptible adjustments; there will be no short turns nor any distances that need quick adjustments. All in all, the very even, smooth round, ridden invisibly, should win. Upon entering the ring (Figure 11), the rider trots up the side of the ring alongside the jumps and picks up his right lead, moves up into his pace, and comes down the center of the ring over a brush. It is better that he jump the brush off the right lead rather than the left because his turn after the brush will be a right turn. He then goes up the side of the ring over a white gate, then 75 feet, which is a forward five strides, to an oxer composed of a chicken coop and a striped rail. He rounds the end of the ring and proceeds down the diagonal over a brush oxer with white rails. This fence is jumped as a single fence off a long approach, the difficulty being in whether or not the rider is accurate with his eye for a distance. He proceeds around the next end of the ring and again must measure his fence off a long approach at the end of the long side. This time it is a vertical in-and-out built out of natural brown rails, with a distance of 25 feet between. He rounds the next end and finishes down the diagonal over a log fence and brown rail, spread 3 feet, and then 82 feet, which will ride a steady six strides, to a stone wall. You can see that this is a very fluid course with few interruptions and only two related distances, from fence 2 to 3, and from fence 7 to 8. A lot is asked of the rider's eye for a distance out of the galloping stride, which is really what hunter riding is all about. Any abrupt changes or roughness will be particularly noticeable on the course due to the ample space between the jumps. All in all, the discrete, soft, light rider should have the edge in this course, whereas over our Medal course the positive, reactive, strong horseman should come through. Needless to say, it is extremely conceivable that the same rider could possess all these traits and win both classes back to back.

In recent years there has been a growing interest in equitation com-

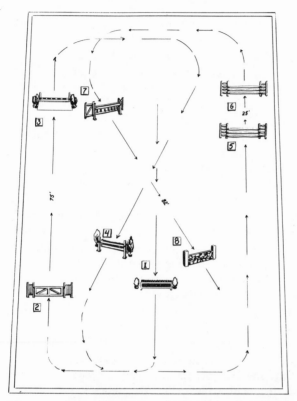

Fig. 11. Course for ASPCA Maclay. (1) brush, 3'6"; (2) white gate, 3'6"; (3) coop and rail oxer, 3'3" and 3'6" x 3'0"; (4) brush and rail oxer, 3'0" and 3'6" x 3'0"; (5) brown rails, 3'6"; (6) brown rails, 3'6" (25' combination); (7) log fence and brown rail oxer, 3'3" and 3'6" x 3'0'" (8) stone wall, 3'6".

petition for riders age eighteen and over. The establishment in 1977 of the Professional Horsemen's Association National Equitation Championship for Adult Riders is recognition of this growth. As in the case of classes for Riders Under Fourteen, these adult classes vary greatly in the skill of the riders.

In some cases, a class will consist almost entirely of young riders who have only recently graduated from the Junior ranks and who were riding in Medal and Maclay classes only a year or so ago. In other cases, a class may consist of riders mostly in their late twenties or in their thirties or older who are not able to ride regularly but who still enjoy competing from time to time. In areas where there is a great deal of interest in adult equitation, the competitions are often divided into classes for those eighteen to twenty-five or thirty and for those twenty-five or thirty and over.

If, as the course designer, I know the majority of riders in an adult equitation class are going to be those who have recently been riding in Junior classes, I would use a course such as I have suggested for an Intermediate or Open class for juniors. The specifications for the National PHA Adult Hunter Seat Equitation Class call for a course of eight or more fences about 3 feet 6 inches in height, with at least one combination, including an oxer, and two changes of direction. The course I have suggested for an Open class would fit this competition well. But for a class for older riders, or for one in which the skill of the riders is very varied, a Limit course would be more in order, but with fences up to 3 feet 3 inches.

I have not placed the USET class with these other classes on purpose. The USET class was introduced into the equitation division several years ago as a test with an added dimension to prepare riders for international competition. The need for this, like the figure-eight course for the Medal, has become a bit lost because the level of riding in all equitation classes has become so sophisticated in recent years. The equitation division has caught up to the USET class. Any Open horsemanship rider is now expected to do (and can be asked in a test) what five years ago was only in the realm of the USET class. Nonetheless, in writing this article, I still feel it necessary to segregate this competition, not lump it in with the others, as that was the original intent, to provide a class with a bit more scope.

The purpose of the USET class, as intended, is a preparation for young riders to go on from their hunter seat work into one or more of the three phases of international competition: dressage, three-day events, or stadium jumping. In these equestrian endeavors it is most important that both horse and rider have a sound background in basic dressage. Therefore one phase of the USET class requires the riders to work on the flat and show their ability in this area in a manner which five years ago was considerably more sophisticated than any other flat work expected of these young riders. Riders are also called on to jump a course of at least ten fences 3 feet 6 inches to 3 feet 9 inches in height, with spreads to 5 feet. If wings are used, they shall be no wider than 36 inches. The course must include a double and a treble combination with at least one spread fence in each and a third spread fence is required elsewhere on the course. Nowadays the only added difficulty in this course at many of the bigger shows is the height. Different problems can be found in the other Open classes throughout the division. Another

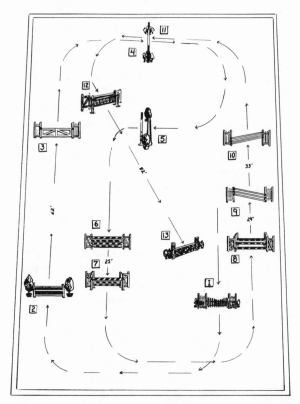

Fig. 12.   Course for USET Class. (1) narrow garden gate, 3'6"; (2) brush and white rail oxer, 3'0" and 3'6" x 3'0"; (3) white gate, 3'9"; (4, 11) vertical rails, 3'6"; (5) stone wall oxer, 3'6" and 3'6" x 3'6"; (6) vertical rails, 3'6"; (7) triple bar planks, 3'0", 3'6", and 3'9" x 4'0" (25' combination); (8) triple bar rails, 2'6", 3'0", and 3'6" x 3'0'" (9) slanted rails, 3'6" (24' combination); (10) slanted rails, 3'6" (33' combination); (12) log oxer, 3'9", 3'9", and 3'9"; (13) stone wall, 3'9".

difference in this class is that standing martingales may not be used. Since martingales are standard equipment for a large number of equitation riders, those riders who depend on them may face problems.

In building my USET course, I am definitely going to stretch the riders in a jumper direction, as that was always the intent of having the competition. On entering the ring (Figure 12), the rider trots up the side alongside the jumps and picks up his right lead. His first fence is a narrow picket gate down the quarter line of the ring. He proceeds around the end of the ring and jumps an oxer made up of brush and white rails, then 62 feet, which divide into four long strides, to a vertical white gate. Set on the middle of the short side of the next end of the ring is a vertical rail fence followed by a half turn to the right over a stone wall oxer, followed immediately by a sharp left-angle turn down the quarter line of the ring over a double combination composed of a vertical plank jump as the first element and a triple bar plank jump as the second, 25 feet apart. After rounding the next end of the ring he comes to our triple combination, a triple bar made up of rails coming in, a vertical of slanted rails 24 feet away, followed by another vertical of slanted rails 33 feet away. After jumping the vertical at the end of the ring going the other direction, he turns left down the diagonal of the ring over a square oxer built around a log gate, followed 82 feet away by a stone wall. This last distance necessitates shortening the horse's stride a bit.

One can see that this course is quite demanding of the rider in three ways: first, the size of the fences; second, the distance adjustments; and third, the quick succession of turns. Surely one must have a responsive, obedient horse to jump this course smoothly and correctly.

To sum up our section of classes and courses for different stages of hunter seat riding, one can see that the important thing is to build and prepare these young riders slowly and carefully to be able to cope with what they will be faced with in showing the hunter and jumper. Let me repeat that I do not feel the equitation division to be an end in itself, only a preparatory division. And when one builds courses one must take this into consideration and offer the right kind of variety. Also it is most important when designing courses to be sure problems and not traps are set: this is as important for the novice rider coming along as it is for the young horse. That is why I really do believe an experienced horseman is the only one who really understands how to build good courses — he has ridden and understands the animal and how best to ride him. All in all, good course building requires knowledge, imagination, and common sense. Only through building constructive courses is it possible to change and develop both horse and rider for the better.

Types of Fences and Their Construction

As you can see from my discussion so far, any and all types of jumps that are generally used for hunter or jumper classes are permissible and suitable for equitation. The name "hunter seat equitation" can be misleading unless one remembers that it is the kind of seat used for any hunter-jumper work, both on the flat and over fences (versus stock seat, saddle seat, dressage seat, and so on). There are still some people who insist that a hunter seat should relate just to the riding of hunters, and therefore hunter seat equitation riders should just jump hunter type courses and obstacles. I disagree. Jumper riding was, and is, an off-shoot of riding horses across country to hounds over various obstacles. Originally, competitions between fox hunting men and their horses were the first so-called jumper events. I will always feel that hunter and jumper classes come from the same mold and that to ride either, the seat should be called the same — hunter seat. I realize that this paragraph reiterates what I said at the outset, but I feel very strongly about reinforcing my point on definition for the people who still are not sure what hunter seat equitation should cover. It covers, in my opinion, any work done on either the hunter or the jumper, and therefore any conventional hunter or jumper type fence is permissible in course building for equitation classes.

The single most important factor in building any jump is that it be well defined. By that I mean that any single piece of equipment is visible enough for both horse and rider to see clearly in order to judge it accurately. Take a rail, for example. There is nothing more unpleasant to approach than a flimsy little stick, 6 feet long and ½ inch in diameter. For instance, offset bamboo rapping poles are often very thin, so the horse does not get a good perspective on them. A rail should be 12 feet long and 4 inches in diameter, at least. It also should be of a bright or deep enough color to be well defined, not one of those poles that blends into the background. And a brush fence should have a nice, sturdy wooden frame and plenty of thick brush stuffed in it — not a few straggly branches waving out of the top. A chicken coop is best solid, not built out of slats with lots of daylight coming through.

Fences, for the most part, should have body. They should not be airy. If a vertical rail fence is built, be sure that enough rails are used to give the obstacle definition. Of course, for a little variety I have no objection to the single rail, providing the rail used is large and brightly painted, with a ground line perhaps of low flower or brush boxes. A solid fence such as a wall topped by a rail, as in Figure 13, is fine. Be sure again, however, that there is not a lot of daylight between the solid obstacle and the rail, or between each rail if more than one is used. Figure 4 gives an example of a poor fence because there is too much daylight between the wall sections and the rail. Six inches should be the maximum between rails, and 3 to 4 inches' separation is much better.

A vertical rail fence with an inch or two between each rail is a lovely, defined jump, but how many horse shows could afford so many rails and cups! What one wants to strive for in building fences is solid definition and not an airy, vague look that invites a miscalculation.

Figs. 13 and 14. The fences above are excellent examples of well-built equitation fences. They are solid, inviting, well framed, and attractive! (Photos by Budd.)

Framing a jump, to me, is most important, more so in show courses perhaps than in schooling at home. At the very least, standards should be used to frame a fence, and quarter wing type standards 30 to 36 inches wide are even better. There is nothing more unattractive than jumping a wall or a coop just stuck out nowhere, without something added a bit higher to frame each end of the fence. It must be so for the horse, too, creating some insecurity, as we have all seen many run-outs at unframed jumps. In fact, for advanced equitation classes, putting in an occasional fence without this frame is a surprise and an excellent test of control. In general, though, I would say it borders a bit on the gim- micky side and really does not enhance the look of the course. We have at our disposal to use as frames not only regulation standards and quarter wing type standards (the old-fashioned long wing takes up too much room and is of course too long to be permitted as a wing in all the open

Fig. 15. A good example of using spruce trees to decorate a fence while also giving greater definition to the frame of the fence. (Photo by Budd.)

Fig. 16. This is a very inviting and jumpable fence for an equitation course. The box on the ground topped by a filled brush box in front of the gate and rail invites a horse to stand back and jump out of stride. The use of outhouses as wing standards not only frames the fence well but gives variety to the course. (Photo by Budd.)

equitation classes) but also all kinds of pillars for walls and trees and shrubs. (See Figures 13–16 for examples of various kinds of frames for fences. It is most attractive if the wing frames match the pattern of the fence, as for example the wall material against the quarter wings in Figure 13, or the wishing wells tied into the wall in Figure 14.) Natural foliage of this type not only sets off the individual fence well but also does wonders in decorating the ring. The only thing one must watch in using trees and bushes is that they are not so high and luxurious as to block off the judges' view. This actually happened at a Medal final and was a very disconcerting factor to the judges that particular year (see Figure 15).

The word "inviting" is often used to describe a nice, jumpable fence, and a good word it is, too. Several factors that we have mentioned already invite horse and rider to approach one fence and not another. Is the jump wide or is it narrow? Is there a frame? Is it a substantial jump with good body or is it flimsy? How about a good ground line, a rail, brush, or flower boxes clearly defining the bottom of the jump from the approach side? Is the fence in good lighting or is it under a shadow? What about the footing coming to the fence? Is there a spooky surrounding to the fence such as an umbrella or judge's stand? There are so many little things that can make some jumps on a course psychologically appealing and others just not. It is really amazing to watch a class and make note of all the errors committed over a certain fence that just is not as inviting as the others. A good course builder makes sure he invites the rider to enter the ring.

Colors are important too. They should be bright, rich, and deep, not pale, garish, or off-color. A good friend of mine decided to do away with tradition and help his horse show along by painting the jumps in far-out colors: purples, pinks, pale greens, and other pastels. It just did not work. Use a good-quality paint and perhaps have the odd panel or wall an off-beat color or pattern rather than making that the norm. Coordinating colors with taste is also a point to remember. Either match all the rails in building a fence or alternate two colors, colors that go well together, not, for instance, orange and red. Do not forget that when using natural rails they should not be mixed with brighter rails or brighter solid fences. A white gate with a brown rail or a striped panel topped by such a rail would be a very poor choice visually (Figure 17). Rustic jumps are most attractive and can be very inviting provided an odd, bright, artificial piece is not thrown in. (See Figures 10A and 10B in Chapter 1 for illustrations of excellent rustic fences.) Take lighting into account, too, and keep the dark, natural-colored fences out of dark spots on the course. Light-colored fences may be placed anywhere but dark

Fig. 17. These two fences in combination are a good illustration of the effect that can be created by coordinating the coloring of standards, rails, and panels. The flower boxes help define the ground lines, and the shrubs widen the frames. Fences in combination should be constructed so that they harmonize. (Photo by Budd.)

ones need that good lighting. One last thing about colors: fences fade from year to year, and there is nothing quite so good as a fresh coat of paint.

The variety of fences used has always been very important in my evaluation of a course designer. A good course builder always uses his imagination and prevents dullness in his ring by varying the types of jumps and their presentation. A combination of colors and materials along with interesting, unusual jumps helps liven things up. Of course the show that is constantly searching for and providing new fences for its course designer is much more helpful to him than one in which he has nothing to work with but the same old things. There are many different types of walls and coops, for instance. Gates come in all shapes, sizes, and widths. Most anything can be done with painted panels, and the variety of fences one can build with rails is almost limitless. A really serious course designer should keep a file of diagrams or photographs of every fence he has ever seen in a show ring or schooling paddock. Variety is so important. Change, do not forget, is very stimulating both for horse and rider.

While talking on variety, it brings to mind what are called "traps." A trap is an obstacle that is unfair and perhaps impossible for a horse to jump. While striving for variety, be most careful that a jump does not fall into this trap category. The most common form of trap is the false ground line, a rail, or brush box that has been set behind the top element of the jump, causing the horse to jump a little late and probably hit the fence. A spread fence with the far obstacle being set lower than the near one would also fall into this category. Colors and lighting can create traps. For instance, a brown, natural-looking rail on top of a bright, painted one would not be very fair, nor would a darkly painted in-and-out placed in dark, shadowy lighting. Distances between jumps very often succeed in trapping the horse. One must not only plan ridable distances between combinations of fences but also between any two fences with a related distance. There is no surer way of inviting a wreck than to have a distance ride badly between jumps. Poor footing or changeable footing can make a nice jump hazardous, so even where one places jumps in the ring is important. Jumping into the ring rail is bad, as is putting a spread in a position where the landing room is tight. Probably nothing offends the exhibitor more than asking his horse to jump traps. It is really inexcusable to place a trap on a course. But do not confuse problems with traps. A problem is a fence or line of fences that poses a difficulty but a fair one, while a trap is something that simply is not fair to ask a horse to jump. Problems are what courses are all about; traps are not.

Before finishing let me say a word about lighting. Lighting has made or broken many a good class. Good lighting really has only to do with brightness and lack of shadows. During the day shadows can be created outdoors by large trees and during the evening by poorly placed lighting. I think there is nothing more unfair than to ask a horse to perform boldly and smoothly when he is not sure where he is going. Even some indoor rings spook horses just because of the poor quality of lighting. So check lighting and pay a lot of attention to it. In designing your course, keep in mind the time of day when the course will be jumped to avoid having a horse jumping into the bright sun, impairing his view of a fence. In short, a lighting problem should not become a riding problem.

In summing up my discussion regarding fences and their construction, let me say that many specific ingredients go into building a good course. It is really a study for those who have some background as horsemen and are interested in course designing. A person who is lazy and wants to just throw up a course should not be doing this job, nor should someone who really has little experience himself in riding over jumps. As far as I am concerned, courses are tremendously responsible for the quality of performance and also for the development, good or bad, of horse or rider. There is really no way of improving this conception of good riding principles without setting proper courses. Bad riding systems have developed and thrived for years by people going over and over courses that are poor. Take the time necessary to learn about jumps, their construction and placement. Learn about rings, footing, and lighting; become an amateur landscapist and designer. All these aspects go into the development of good show riding as we know it today.

Courses for Hunters

CHRYSTINE JONES HOGAN

Chrystine Jones Hogan. Though only thirty years old, Chrys Jones Hogan, a resident of Birmingham, Michigan, has had an active and varied career with horses. She began riding at the age of six, and among her early instructors were Violet Hopkins, Chuck Grant, Emmy Grant Temple, Robert Egan, and Gabor Foltenyi. A successful rider of both hunters and jumpers, in 1965 she won the national finals of both the AHSA Medal and the ASPCA Maclay competitions. That year she also joined the jumping squad of the U.S. Equestrian Team, riding Ksarina. As a team member she won the Grand Prix of Cologne in 1966, and the following year was the Leading Lady Rider of that show. In 1967 she also won the President's Cup at the Washington International.

Mrs. Hogan became a professional in 1971 and has won distinction since as a trainer and instructor, as a judge, and as a designer of both jumper and hunter courses. Among the major shows where she has been course designer one or more times are Detroit, Oakbrook, the National in New York, Eastern States, Children's Services, Houston, the Jacksonville Classic, and the American Royal. She is presently a director of the AHSA and chairman of the AHSA's Junior Hunter-Jumper Committee.

Hunter Competition in America

Show ring hunter classes evolved from the nineteenth-century practice of fox hunt members gathering at a farm site to compare their mounts in informal competition. At horse shows during the early 1900s, specific events for fox hunters were offered, such as those for light, middle, and heavyweight horses, for qualified hunters that had been regularly ridden with a pack of hounds recognized by the Masters of Foxhounds Association of America (or England), for Corinthian hunters ridden in formal hunting attire by an amateur member of a recognized hunt, for ladies' hunters, for Thoroughbred and non-Thoroughbred horses, and for hunter hacks that performed both on the flat and over fences.

Today's show hunter, however, is a lighter-weight, better-moving version of the typical fox hunter of yesteryear and is rarely used for hunting purposes. And, because of the requirements in the qualified and Corinthian events and the sex discrimination in the ladies' classes, many of these competitions have been discontinued at recognized shows, although they are still common in hunter trials and small local shows.

The American Horse Shows Association currently recognizes hunter classes in the following categories: Hunter Breeding, Green and Regular Conformation, Green and Regular Working, Amateur-Owner, Junior, and Pony Hunters. In addition, shows may offer miscellaneous classes for pairs, hunt teams, bridle path hacks, novice hunters, and so forth, depending on local interest. The Canadian Horse Shows Association recognizes similar categories of competition, with essentially the same requirements. Recognized shows must include one under-saddle class and a specified number of over-fences classes in each section offered, according to their AHSA rating (except in the Hunter Breeding Division). In the over-fences events, hunters are judged on their performance and soundness of limb, wind, and vision. Performance includes the maintenance of an even hunting pace, manners, jumping style, and way of moving over the course. A hunter course should therefore be designed to encourage an even-paced, faultless performance and should be carefully planned and measured to accommodate the modern hunter's flowing, natural stride. The term "jumping style" refers to the form of the horse during takeoff, flight, and landing. Ideally, a hunter should seek the center of an obstacle and jump in a balanced arc over the top, without drifting to the side or twisting the torso. The legs should be neatly drawn up, knees folded well up in front, and hocks bent behind; neither end should be left dangling. A horse that naturally has good style will perform consistently over flat or rolling terrain, vertical or spread fences. Again, the course should be designed to encourage horses to jump in perfect form and not cause any unnecessary contortions. Less talented horses will be observed by the judge and placed accordingly. A hunter course designer need not create a difficult "test" for hunters but, rather, should endeavor to build a course that produces good performances. A judge's job is much easier if there are several faultless rounds in a class, allowing the judge to determine who the winners are based on their style and way of going rather than considering those who committed the least number of errors.

Courses and Requirements
for Different Hunter Competitions

Frequently, observers have noted that the Novice and First Year Green Sections are notably larger than the Second Year and Regular Working Sections. The most obvious reason is that many horses do not have the ability to go on to jump greater heights. It may well be, however, that many of these youngsters were exposed to too many awkward distances and poorly constructed fences and that they consequently lost their confidence and style. Courses for young horses should consist of simple lines that embolden them to remain calm and to jump in good form. Inaccurate distances between fences that require sudden acceleration or result in a last-second "stabbed in" stride will eventually cause a horse to jump quickly and flat or refuse altogether, having completely lost heart. Distances for the novice horse, jumping 3 feet 3 inches or less, should be calculated on a 12-foot stride. This length of stride is quite comfortable for a young horse and, therefore, makes it relatively easy to get from one fence to the next on the same line.

A line of fences, two (or more) related obstacles in a row, and the relation of one line to the next are very important factors in designing

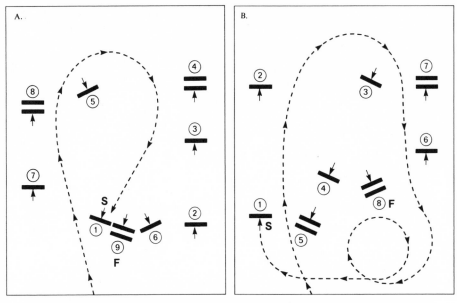

Fig. 1. A horse and rider tend to proceed directly to the first fence when it is to be jumped going toward the in-gate, *A,* but will tour the arena *and* make a circle when the first fence is going away from the gate, *B.* During a show session, many precious minutes are lost on the latter pattern.

courses for young hunters. In an arena, oval or rectangle, the only way to reverse direction without disturbing the cadence of the horse is across the diagonals — never across the center or on a serpentine. I have found that starting green horses over the first fence going *toward* the in gate rather than away helps develop their pace and confidence before approaching the first line of fences in the course (see Figure 1). The in-and-out should come later in the course and be the last segment of a line of fences; it should never be the second fence of the course. For example, off of a turn, the first fence in a line might be an inviting, sloping vertical, followed by an even 12-foot-stride distance — let us say 60 feet — to a simple in-and-out comprised of a vertical fence placed as the "in" and a narrow oxer as the "out." The reason for placing a spread at the out location is to discourage a green hunter from trying to exit the series too quickly, thereby jumping in a flat, out-of-balance form. Small oxers may be incorporated throughout the course, but these spreads for hunters should never be "square"; that is, the front element should be 3 to 6 inches lower (preferably 6 inches) than the back. Placement is important. An oxer is more impressive for a novice than a seasoned mount and is better placed as the last segment of a line or singly with a long approach. Extreme care must be used when building an oxer immediately following a turn, inasmuch as it may surprise a youngster whose attention is wandering or is, due to lack of experience, slow to seek the fence on a curve.

On an outside course, a designer has more options creating lines that result in a change of direction. In a large area, turns through the center, S-shaped, and half-turns are all workable patterns. Even one large circle of fences, jumped on the same lead, is acceptable — although unimaginative. In any case, it must be stressed that the lines should follow a gently curving design that does not force the horse to execute an abrupt turn or acute angle to an obstacle.

The stride of the horse must be considered in designing a course, as I shall explain below. Figure 2 illustrates how one counts strides between fences.

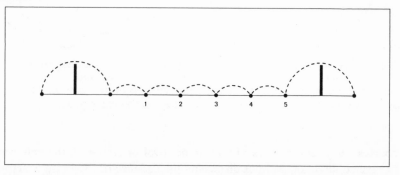

Fig. 2. Counting Strides between Fences. Note that the first stride is counted as marked and not when the horse's front legs hit the ground on the landing side of the fence.

When designing courses for ponies in an arena, one should pay careful attention to the peculiar strides for small-, medium-, and large-sized ponies, and take the time and effort necessary to adjust the distance between fences accordingly. Basically, the measurements are determined on stride lengths of 9 feet for small, 10 feet for medium, and 11 feet for large ponies. It is best to establish the desired number of strides based on a standard 12-foot distance and then subtract the number of feet less per stride based on the size of the pony (small, 3 feet per stride; medium, 2 feet per stride; large, 1 foot per stride). Attempting to establish a distance between fences based on dividing the total footage by strides becomes quite confusing when trying to allow for takeoff and landing space.

Table 1. Distances Between Fences for Ponies (in feet)

Number of Strides	Small	Medium	Large
1	20	22	24
2	30	32	34
3	39	42	45
4	48	52	56
5	57	62	67
6	66	72	78
7	75	82	89

If, in a given division, the competition consists of high-quality, fluid moving ponies, these distances may be increased slightly to suit the naturally longer strides. The table is, however, a useful point of reference in establishing distances for ponies, keeping in mind variances such as uphill and downhill grades, mud, and so on. When the measurements are beyond 82 feet in the arena, it is no longer necessary to calculate the striding for the small and medium sections, because they will have enough stride options over a longer stretch.

Another important suggestion to those designing courses for ponies is to keep in mind the age of the youngsters in the saddle. Although many are seasoned campaigners by the age of ten, others are just beginning their careers as riders and, in most cases, they are all experiencing the "butterflies." One of the most unhappy sights I have ever witnessed occurred at a large horse show a few years ago. A girl of approximately eight years of age was mounted on her pony awaiting her turn to perform. The course was long, winding, and consisted of twelve obstacles! As the trainer and family were grilling her about the proposed route, panic set in. At that tender age, the poor, nervous child simply could not retain the complicated plan in her head and she burst into tears. Scenes such as that are disheartening indeed. Designers must avoid building courses that are too complicated or obstacles that are too difficult for the young exhibitor (see Figure 3). It is very important to encourage the budding, young rider through a positive experience in the show ring.

Junior and amateur exhibitors also merit special consideration. A junior rider in a children's hunter section may, like the pony exhibitor, be a newcomer to the sport and need to gain confidence as well as mileage. Distances between obstacles should be calculated on a 12-foot stride, as for novice green hunters, allowing the horse and rider to arrive at their take-off point in a calm, even pace (see Figure 4). Usually, the height for children's hunters is 3 feet and, therefore, the arc and flight of

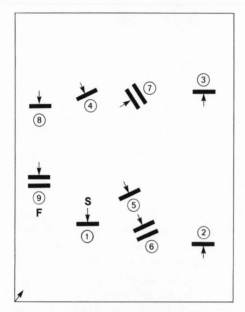

Fig. 3.   Sample Novice Hunter Course. Note that all the in-and-outs are jumped going toward the in-gate end of the arena rather than away. To further simplify this course, one or both of the combinations could be removed or changed to simple lines of fences.

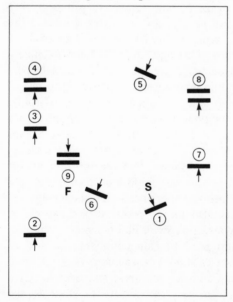

Fig. 4.   Sample Junior or Amateur Hunter Course in arena. In-and-outs nos. 3 and 4, nos. 7 and 8, are 26 feet and 38 feet respectively.

the horse is minimal. In-and-out measurements of 24 feet for one stride and 36 feet for two strides generally work well in an arena. These distances may be increased slightly if the competition is taking place on an outside course.

Older junior riders who are capable of riding in the open equitation division have more control and self-assurance and are probably better mounted for the stiffer competition. At 3-foot-6-inch heights, these competitors can easily handle distances computed on a 12-foot-6-inch to 13-foot stride. Occasionally, use of the 12-foot-6-inch length of stride is preferable. In a small arena, for example, if a line of the first and second fences is to be jumped going away from the in-gate and the second fence of the line is an oxer, the distance calculated on a 12-foot-6-inch stride will ride more comfortably than a 13-foot one. This is due to a combination of factors. First, in a narrow ring it is difficult to develop a galloping pace in making a tight circle before the first fence, and second, riding to an oxer on a line tends to lengthen the distance inasmuch as the horse reaches the apex of his arc over the middle of the spread, not over the front element. Later in the same course, however, a line headed home, toward the in/out-gate, may need to be determined on a 13-foot stride to accommodate the established pace and the horse's desire to return to the gate. In a larger arena, a horse can easily cope with the greater distances due to the longer approach track off the turns and the ability to maintain more pace in those wider turns. A designer should attempt to observe a few performances over the course and make copious notes about the distances and turns. (I file all my charts complete with my observations. It is particularly important to note those diagrams that should *not* be repeated! Old charts are invaluable future references for ring dimensions, topography, or simply to stimulate the mind's creative center when a design deadline is rapidly approaching.)

Generally, amateur riders can handle the same courses as those designated for the open junior division but, again, avoid using twisting courses that have awkward means of approach to the obstacles. Many amateur exhibitors are "weekend" riders and they appreciate an uncomplicated route that produces good performances from their horses and gives them, as well, a confidence-building experience in the show ring. If an amateur division is divided into two subsections at a show, the younger group invariably has greater riding capabilities since they recently graduated from the junior ranks. However, keep in mind when drawing the plans that these two sections usually follow one another in the show time schedule and it is not wise to alter the course between these events. The most successful strategy is to use simple courses that are *easy* for the younger set and *enjoyable* for the seniors. (The exceptions, are, of

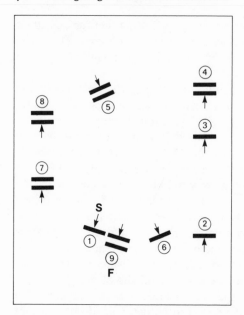

Fig. 5.   Sample Regular Working Hunter Course in arena. In-and-outs nos. 3 and 4, nos. 7 and 8, are 27 feet and 39 feet respectively.

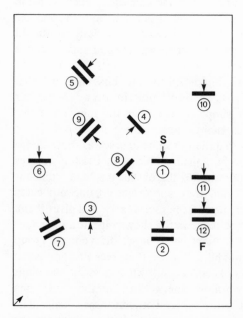

Fig. 6.   Sample Hunter Classic Course. Fences no. 8 and no. 9 and no. 11 and no. 12 are in-and-outs of two strides and one stride respectively.

course, handy classes and classics, which are dealt with later in this section.)

Regular working hunters, at the 4-foot heights, usually have no difficulty with distances based on a 13-foot stride. In calculating these distances, again, it is best to first determine the number of strides and total footage based on the well-known 12-foot stride and then add 1 additional foot for each stride to be taken. Otherwise, it is possible to inadvertently add 1 foot for the take-off/landing space. For example, 72 feet equals five 12-foot strides, and if 1 foot per stride is added, the result is 77 feet. If, however, you divide 72 feet by 12, the resulting figure is 6 . . . but a horse does not take six strides in 72 feet, he takes 5! The reason for the erroneous result is that there must be an allowance for landing and take-off space when measuring between two obstacles on a line. The landing area is not considered as part of stride number 1. The first complete stride taken after a fence is counted as number 1, the second as number 2, and so forth.

At 4-foot heights, if the additional 1-foot length (based on $72 \div 12 = 6$) were added, it would not necessarily be too long, but be very careful about going to a 78-foot distance for juniors and amateurs performing at a 3-foot-6-inch height. Because the arc over a 3-foot-6-inch obstacle is smaller, the resultant distance between two fences could become exceedingly long. (The excepting factor is a downhill grade.) Also, the types of obstacles and their sequence have a major influence on whether or not a measured track requires a long stride.

At most "A" rated horse shows, a 4-foot height is a substantial one for working hunters, certainly for open conformation hunters. If the competition is of particularly high caliber, however, a few 4-foot-3-inch obstacles may be included in the course. The higher, more difficult fence must be placed in a prime location, as, for instance, a sloping oxer that is the last part of a line headed toward the in-gate. This set-up gives all entrants the best possible conditions under which to approach a larger hurdle, but the less talented jumpers will still identify themselves. It is most important to carefully analyze the caliber of the entrants before building a course that is too demanding and creates a poor spectacle.

In hunter classics, the 13-foot-stride increments are usually successful for juniors and amateurs, and the additional 1 foot of overall length also works well for open hunter classics when more fences are 4 feet 3 inches in height, perhaps a few inches wider than normal, and the horses tend to be traveling at a slightly stronger pace. Size of arena, inclines, curving lines, and the location of the first measured line in the course are all factors that can radically affect a ridable measurement and require special consideration. Under such circumstances, the designer's "hunch" is

often the best guideline. When in doubt, use the more conservative calculation, which is safer for the horse and rider.

Classic courses should be slightly longer than the average hunter
course, with a minimum of ten fences. In this type of course, it is quite
common to incorporate two in-and-outs and, perhaps, a line of three
separate obstacles that are four or five strides from one another. A
three-stride distance between fences, or a gently curving line of fences,
add variety to the overall pattern. Nothing tricky. Classics are simply
amplified hunter courses. The fences should be well framed, have clearly
defined ground lines, and be lushly decorated with shrubs and flowers.
A horse maintaining a brisk hand gallop will jump bolder and in more
consistent form over obstacles that are dense in appearance. (Decorating fences has been discussed in Chapters 1 and 2.)

There is no "set" of distances that is foolproof, but the following basic
table is helpful in establishing a logical measurement. From these figures,
a designer can lengthen or shorten the distances depending on the influ-
encing variables.

Table 2.　Distances Between Fences for Horses (in feet)

Number of Strides	3' (Novice Children's)	3'6" (Junior/ Amateur Working)	4' (Open Working)	4'3" (Classics)*
1	25'	26'–27'	27'–27'6"	28'
2	36'	37'–37'6"	38'	39'
3	48'	49'–50'	51'	52'
4	60'	62'–63'	64'	65'
5	72'	75'–76'	77'	78'
6	84'	87'–88'	90'	91'
7	96'	99'6"–100'	103'	104'

* The figures listed are the *maximum* lengths that an even galloping hunter can
handle, and should be used judiciously.

Planning the Course

The first step in designing courses for a show is to determine the exact
size of the arenas (or areas) and the location of the entry and exit gates.
I occasionally will request a topographical map if the area is extremely
hilly or intersected by a road, ditch, or trees. First, all distinguishing
landmarks should be accurately sited on the ring diagrams before assign-

ing obstacle locations. Second, study the sequence of classes in the time schedule to determine the time needed for height, distance, and design alterations. For example, during a day-long session, an outside hunter course may need only changes in height, whereas an arena scheduled for a wide variety of events may require constant modifications of courses. In such a case, it is wise to design a course that can be jumped in several different patterns to fulfill AHSA course change requirements and avoid wasting time on construction. If lengthy lunch and/or dinner recesses are provided for in the schedule, a designer may allocate that time for an elaborate change in the design of the course.

Third, it is also important to ascertain the amount of time it will take a horse to negotiate each course, based on the travel rate of 360 yards per minute. Some courses can be negotiated in 60 seconds (including entry and exit time), while other designs may take over 2 minutes' running time per horse. The location of the start and the finish and their relation to the arena gates, the overall number of lines and directional changes, refusals, and repair of broken equipment are all factors that affect the timely running of a show. If an event has a multitude of contestants, a designer should create a course that expedites the conduct of the class while still complying with class specifications. An interesting observation is that a horse and rider take less time to commence a course when the first fence is jumped heading toward, rather than away from, the in-gate since the rider usually guides his mount to the far end of the arena and then proceeds directly to fence number 1. In the opposite situation, the horse will still be ridden to the far end (unless ordered not to do so by show management) before returning to the in-gate end and then execute a circle in that area before approaching the first fence. The second pattern takes longer and can waste precious minutes during a heavily scheduled session.

In designing courses for arenas, it is essential to draw the course on graph paper rather than plain note paper, napkins, paper plates . . . I've seen it all! Graph paper is made in many different sizes, and all are workable. I prefer 10 squares to the inch because it can be easily scaled to fit any size arena and still allow marginal space for notations such as the class number, title, and date. By utilizing the graph, accurately divided into feet per inch, a course designer can eliminate many lastminute embarrassing alterations and unnecessary delays in construction time. If a design does not fit on the graph plan, then it will not fit into the arena. It is as simple as that. All the wishful thinking in the world won't change that fact. So, save that clever new design for a show with a larger ring and go on to another concept for the current project. For each obstacle, draw in the total length of the fence, including both wings.

Accurate measurements on the graph plan save time and eliminate aggravation at the show. When possible, mark the sides of the arena and the graph plan in corresponding 10-foot sections. This procedure will expedite locating and unloading equipment at the proper obstacle positions.

It is not necessary to have an inventory of equipment when initially planning the course diagrams for a show, though it certainly helps. If the show is renting equipment from a reputable company, there should be plenty of material to work with at the show site. Some horse shows have their own equipment. In most cases, it is in need of repair and sadly outdated. It would behoove a designer to request a list of equipment, complete with dimensions, from any show using its own inventory. All hanging equipment, poles, gates, and planks should be of the same length, and should be slightly longer than base material such as walls, coops, logs, and brush boxes. A new coat of paint will improve an old inventory, and a course designer should confirm with show management that all equipment will be in excellent condition. The linear diagrams should be prepared before a designer departs for a show. At the show site, the inventory must be carefully examined to confirm lengths of material and to note pieces that are in compatible colors. Finally, the equipment is assigned to the fences on the diagram.

Course plans should consist of direct, uncomplicated lines with smooth changes of direction, excepting a handy hunter course. All hunter courses are comprised of sides, diagonals, and, occasionally, a line up the center if the size of the show area and the pattern of the course can accommodate such a line without interrupting the rhythm of the horse's gallop. There are an infinite number of variations in design while still complying with the guidelines, as seen in Figures 1–7. Large areas, designated as an outside course, allow more flexibility in design, always keeping in mind the relation of one line of fences to the next. Although a change in direction is not mandatory, it does give the judge the opportunity to observe the horse's performance on both leads. If the area has an uneven topography, then that factor, alone, will determine the placement of obstacles. It is important to locate oxers and in-and-outs on relatively level sections of ground and to avoid placing even a single fence on a severe incline or immediately following a dip or unusual strip, such as a gravel path, which might alter the horse's stride while in a final approach to an obstacle.

Today's course plans continually become more sophisticated as the caliber of show horses improves. It is not unusual to see a hunter course consisting of up to ten obstacles, including two in-and-outs and several sloping oxers. Again, the amount of time allotted to a class and the ability of the competitors have bearing on the elaboration of the course.

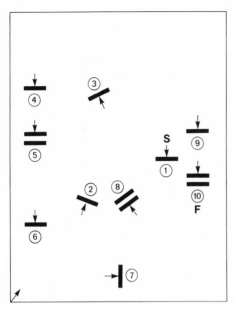

Fig. 7. Sample Handy Hunter Course. Fence no. 7 should be designated as a trot fence. All handy courses in recognized AHSA divisions must contain a fence to be negotiated in the trot as well as an in-and-out. In this diagram fences no. 4 and no. 5 are a one-stride in-and-out and no. 9 and no. 10 are a two-stride combination. The turn from no. 8 to no. 9 offers a nice option to riders depending on the handiness of their mount.

Classes offering a large amount of prize money, such as classics, should also have more demanding course plans.

Special courses such as those for handy hunters, pairs, and hunt teams have distinctive specifications. Guidelines for these events will be set forth in the show prize list, but requirements should be cross-checked with the AHSA rule book. The rule book currently states that a "handy course must have at least two changes of direction and at least one combination; horses are required to trot over one fence toward the end of the course and may be asked to lead over one fence" (see Figure 7). All too often, there is only one change of direction, or the combination is omitted. Riders are rarely required to dismount and lead over a fence because it consumes too much time, as does any peculiar test such as crossing a simulated bridge or opening a gate. If a "lead-over" fence is to be used, it should be the final obstacle and be no higher than 2 feet, so that the rider can easily vault over it and does not need to remount.

Instructions to exit the arena dismounted should be clearly posted on the exhibitors' course diagram.

The word "handy" means to be ready or adroit. A handy class is not a test of brawn, and the rider's hands should not be forced to jerk right and left on the horse's mouth while attempting to execute hairpin turns into fences or to halt abruptly inside a combination. The course should, however, contain several optional turns and a point of transition to the trot where the horse and rider may demonstrate dexterity and promptness.

Pair classes may require horses to perform either abreast or in tandem. Double-paneled fences should be used for abreast pairs to avoid an in-flight accident. If a show cannot provide two identical panels for each fence, then the class should be conducted under the tandem specifications, and the course designer should mark on the diagram where the horses should exchange positions. Although when in tandem they do not perform side by side, the horses enter and exit the arena abreast. A hunt team enters the arena abreast as a team of three and then peels off single file in the circle prior to the first fence. They may be required to jump the last fence abreast, but only if the designer has enough material to build three identical sections, and this must also be clearly indicated on the posted diagram.

It is always shrewd to refer to the rule book when drafting courses for any division or special classes, especially hunter classics, to make certain all rules and technicalities are properly adhered to; for nothing irritates an exhibitor more than having had class points nullified due to an illegal course.

Types of Obstacles

Obstacles can be separated into two categories: verticals and spreads. Within each category are many variations. A vertical fence may be a "true" vertical (in an absolute vertical line from top to bottom) or a sloping vertical, even to the extent of becoming a ramp, the latter being undesirable. A spread fence consists of multiple verticals or a wider plane that is jumped as one unit. Oxers, Liverpools, and ditches are hunter obstacles that are classified as spreads. Triple bars are not suitable for hunters, although a triple bar effect can be created by using a combination of different height boxes and poles (see Figure 23). Oxers for hunters should not be the same height in front and behind, commonly referred to as "square." A square oxer tests the horse's ability to collect his weight in the hindquarters and to execute a greater arc over the top of the fence, and is a test more appropriate for jumpers than hunters.

Fig. 8. Chicken Coop and Pole. This fence is not properly constructed since it lacks a well-defined ground line and is not framed with wings. The ground line could be improved by placing a thin layer of loose fir along the base. A standing flower box should not be used here because the sloping front of the coop and the vertical sides of the ground box are incompatible.

Fig. 9. Chicken Coop and Pole. This fence has good ground fill and is well framed but note that the bottom pole is difficult to see and creates an illusion that the fence is "off-set," i.e., the top rail protrudes more toward the front of the fence. It is important to use evenly matched poles. (Photo by Rosemary Ruppert.)

A hunter should not be asked to shorten and collect his stride to that degree, but rather to meet the fences in a natural, hand-galloping stride. Therefore, with that objective, the best types of fences to incorporate in most hunter courses are verticals and spreads with sloping façades. Occasionally, a straight-fronted vertical can be used to test the well-seasoned working horse, but a true vertical is not necessary inasmuch as the designer is not compelling a hunter to knock a rail down.

All hunter fences should have plenty of material and appear to be solid. It is dangerous, however, to make a fence top-heavy by placing an extremely fat pole over a series of thin poles. On the other hand, it is unfair to place a flimsy pole on top that is too easily knocked down.

Rail fences should be uniformly constructed with straight, round-edged poles that are approximately 4 inches in diameter at both ends. The gap between hung poles should never exceed 9 inches. Poles for hunters can be natural, such as cedar or birch, or painted common colors like brown, rust, or white. Striped poles should not be used — not even in hunter classics!

It is possible to create a variety of fences within this limited color spectrum. In addition to poles, fill-in material may include planks (solid or ladder-style) and small gates (flat or picket top). These can be hung over many different base pieces such as brush boxes, walls, logs, coops, and water troughs. These base pieces should be constructed with light-weight board so that they are not difficult to move and can be painted

Fig. 10.   Rails. The difference between a 3″ octagonally cut pole and a 4″ round pole is clearly shown. The round cedar pole on the top is much easier to focus on to determine an accurate perception of depth. (Photo by Rosemary Ruppert.)

Fig. 11.   Gate Oxer. This oxer is too square and airy. The pole on the back element is barely visible, and there is too much space between the bottom of the gate and the ground. The gate should be 3″ to 6″ lower than the rear pole, and since the components of the gate are widely spaced, this fence should have either a substantial flower box in front or be well filled front and center with loose fir. (Photo by Rosemary Ruppert.)

Fig. 12. Stone Wall. A wall should not be slanted on both sides inasmuch as it becomes too broad at the base to be knocked over and may cause a horse to become hung up on top of it. Ideally a wall or coop should be slanted on one side and vertical on the other. Note that although the fence has a well-filled ground line, it still appears somewhat stark due to the lack of potted trees at the wings to create a proper frame. (Photo by Rosemary Ruppert.)

in motifs resembling red brick, gray stone, or log bark. Roll coops are usually painted green or covered with artificial grass to simulate a countryside bank. In today's show ring, it is not uncommon to see the wings of fences mocked up as wishing wells, outhouses, and stone columns. The equipment for hunter courses can be quite charming rather than dull when the inventory is well coordinated and has been artistically decorated by a professional sign painter. It is fundamental that all hanging pieces are the same length, normally 12 feet, and that standing pieces are slightly shorter, about 11 feet, so that a pole, for example, can be hung over a wall and still sit securely in the cups. Cups and pins should be metal and be a minimum of 1½ inches deep and 5 inches across.

A variety of take-off boxes filled with artificial flowers, ivy, or broom-style brushes are useful in sprucing up the ground line of an obstacle or changing its nature altogether. For instance, flower boxes may be placed in front of and on top of a 2-foot red brick wall that has matching pillars with a 2-foot white gate hung at 4 feet behind the base, creating a colorful, solid staircase effect. These boxes are also used to outline a Liverpool panel or to fill the inside of a water trough.

In addition to the artificial embellishments, a show should supply the course designer with a sufficient quantity of potted shrubs 3 feet to 3 feet 6 inches high, in heavy-duty plastic or wooden pots, and loose cut fir.

Fig. 13. Gate Oxer. This rustic gate oxer is well filled and framed and has a distinct difference in height between the front and back elements. The only way of improving this fence would be to replace the separate wing and standard units with the more compact wing standard. (Photo by Rosemary Ruppert.)

All fences should have clearly defined ground lines and, if spread, be filled with fir or potted shrubs inside the spread. The loose fir pieces are a lush finishing touch on the ground lines of solid equipment like walls and coops and create a distinct outline that produces better performances in an event. Trees placed on either side of an obstacle, in front of the wings, help to frame the fence and encourage the horse to jump in the center. If a Liverpool is used, it should not be overly impressive, but must have a well-defined take-off box in front and be silhouetted by dense foliage. These decorative measures discourage a horse from placing a stride in the pool or jumping diagonally out the side.

As soon as the course designer is in possession of the inventory list, the equipment should be assigned to the diagrams. A sample course might be comprised of nine obstacles including two combinations. In most cases, the first fence is a brush box, or boxes, without a pole, and is so noted on the graph. Two different-size brush boxes packed tightly together, the lower in front, produce the desirable sloping façade. The next step is to determine which pairs of fences are compatible as in-and-outs. An unusual but interesting treatment is to break up the equipment that makes up a total single unit such as a 2-foot gray wall with matching columns. The columns are assigned to the "in" fence along with a small white gate, one white pole, and a pair of yellow flower take-off boxes.

The "out" oxer is comprised of the 2-foot matching wall, 2 pairs of white wings, 3 white poles, and a pair of yellow flower take-off boxes. Thus, the combination is composed of two very different obstacles and yet has an overall look of artistic unity. The last phase in assigning fence materials is to complete the individual oxers and verticals. Lines of fences should be pleasing to the eye and not conflicting in color and design. It is especially important to avoid building a blazing conglomeration following a relatively colorless obstacle, thus diverting the horse's attention from the first fence before it has been negotiated. Occasionally, a scheme might be carried throughout a line by using matching flower boxes. Combination fences should be congruent in order to avoid startling a horse after jumping into the set. Finally, allocate the decorative foliage.

Using good judgment, the course designer can experiment with a mixture of equipment. A ladder-style plank over a wall, a gate hung between pillars or wishing wells, and wall blocks under the front element of an oxer are all variations that create a more picturesque course. Another innovation is to use the brush boxes in an oxer, later in the course, and to assign different material to the first fence.

Semipermanent outside courses might be comprised of a slightly different inventory inasmuch as the obstacles are not constantly relocated. Authentic stone walls and hedges, topped off with poles in cups; aikens made of vertical rails and a mound of fir trees; stacked telephone poles or railroad ties and lovely, straight birch poles make beautiful hunter

Fig. 14. Gate Fence for Ponies. Here, a 3'6" gate has been lowered to a 2'6" height for ponies, creating a dangerously severe ramp front that is too wide and invites a pony to gallop up to the front of it. A 2'6" or 3' gate would be more suitable and should replace the larger hunter gate for pony events. (Photo by Rosemary Ruppert.)

Fig. 15. Interlocked Wing Standards. These create a good width of spread for all ponies and novice horses. If the wing is displaced, it can be quickly re-set without remeasuring the spread with a tape. (Photo by Rosemary Ruppert.)

Fig. 16. Wing Standards, "Toe to Toe." Here is a nice width of spread for all hunters other than ponies and novice horses. This spread, like the interlocked fence (Figure 15), can be quickly and accurately re-set without measurement. A spread may be increased to 3'6" for hunter classics, but such a spread must be remeasured each time it is even slightly displaced. (Photo by Rosemary Ruppert.)

Fig. 17. Plank Oxer. Natural or brown planks make a more solid looking fence than just rails alone, but this particular fence also illustrates several design errors. The oxer is too square for hunters, i.e., the front and back should not be the same height but, rather, ascending in height. A single rail on the back of an oxer is not only sufficient, but safer. It is also dangerous to leave extra equipment stored under the rear element, such as the plank on the ground, where a horse might accidentally land or slip on it. (Photo by Rosemary Ruppert.)

fences. A "snake" fence is easily constructed by setting three or more panels of rail verticals at slight angles to one another in a zigzag line. Care must be taken to see that the angles are not too sharp. It is imperative that all fences on an outside course have defined ground lines because the horse and rider are traveling at a greater pace and need to establish an accurate depth perception of each fence.

If a fence has a pleasant, balanced appearance, it is usually well constructed. Some common faults in fence construction for hunters are: lack of or recessed ground lines; airy, insubstantial facades; square or offset oxers; insufficiently filled oxers; improper silhouetting or lack of wings and backward angles on hanging pieces, that is, a gate should slope toward the take-off, not landing, side. The backside of an obstacle should never be overloaded with poles — one is usually sufficient; nor should the back be used as a storage area for extra equipment. It is unsightly and could be injurious to the horse (see Figure 17).

Fig. 18. Take-Off Box. This should never be placed too far out in front of a fence because it may surprise a horse and is also difficult to replace with precision should it be displaced during a refusal or knockdown. The box should be lightly touching the bottom of the gate so that there is no question as to its original placement, and it is always in the same place for every horse in the class. (Photo by Rosemary Ruppert.)

Fig. 19. Ground-Line Box. Placed directly under an obstacle, it creates a "flush" front and is a more difficult fence for a hunter to jump. (Photo by Rosemary Ruppert.)

Pony fences should be built with small pieces of equipment rather than by placing large items on severe angles, creating a ramp, as in Figure 14. Ingenious use of wall blocks, ladders and planks, straw bales, and 2-foot gates can result in a delightful miniature hunter course. Oxers for ponies should be sloping and built with the wing standards "interlocked" rather than "toe to toe" as illustrated in Figures 15 and 16. The interlocked position is narrower and is recommended for ponies, novice, and children's hunters. The wing standards placed toe to toe create an ideal spread for all other hunter divisions. Both positions can be quickly rebuilt without remeasuring. Wider spreads may be utilized in hunter classics but will require careful measurement, and should not exceed 4 feet.

If a show's inventory is limited, it can be supplemented with straw bales, wall blocks, natural and birch poles, artificial funeral grass sheets, and lush underbrush. If potted shrubs are unavailable, dense fir branches can be artfully tied to the wing standards as well as heaped in mounds to fill in oxers. Ground-line boxes can be easily adorned with artificial holiday holly ropes that are very inexpensive in the off-season, and can be securely fastened to the box with a heavy-duty staple gun. A fresh coat of paint on what material there is and an abundance of loose fir can go a long way toward achieving an attractive hunter course.

Fig. 20. Wishing Well and Trough. This new design of wing standard and wall is now widely accepted in hunter events and adds variety and color to a course. (Photo by Darkroom-on-Wheels.)

Fig. 21. A matching set of stone columns and 16″ wall may be used together with a gate and brush take-off box to create a sloping vertical fence. The wall blocks are placed in front of the gate and the brush box on top and at the back edge of the wall, forming a solid staircase effect. This particular wall is also 16″ deep and is about the maximum width I would recommend for a protruding ground line. (Photo by Budd.)

Fig. 22. When two separate fences on a course must be constructed close together, it is sometimes interesting and visually appealing to color co-ordinate them as shown in this photograph. The obstacle on the right is comprised of a rust and yellow wall with matching columns, a rust picket gate, and a pair of yellow flower take-off boxes. On the left is a natural gate and rail oxer with rust wing standards and yellow flower takeoffs. The two fences are quite different in type but compatible in color. Also note the proper use of potted shrubs in front of the wings and in the center of the oxer. (Photo by Budd.)

Fig. 23. Brush Boxes and Poles. A staircase of brush boxes and poles creates a solid-looking slope front that encourages a horse to make a proper arc. Also note how the single wing-standard unit improves the appearance of the fence. (Photo by Rosemary Ruppert.)

Variables

On occasion, a meticulously measured and beautifully constructed course will still contain a place where a large percentage of the participants encounter some difficulty. When the same fence or line of fences continues to present a problem, then it is possible that the course designer has not anticipated the effect of a variable factor. Inclines and muddy ground cause the horse to alter the length of his normal stride and he is therefore unable to arrive at the proper take-off point if the distances have not been adjusted accordingly. A horse's stride is shorter on an ascending slope and longer on a gradually descending slope, although a severe descent will cause the stride to shorten as the horse brakes himself. Muddy conditions or ground hard and slippery like concrete are two extreme circumstances that produce a shorter length of stride. The footing in an indoor ring should be carefully examined for soft spots or wet areas. Most horses will attempt to jump an obvious wet spot, and a fence should not be constructed with such a spot directly in the line of approach.

Other factors worth consideration are those that affect the horse's vision and perception. The eye of a horse does not adapt to darkness or sudden changes of illumination as quickly as the human eye. This fact, alone, may account for numerous refusals at the first fence in an enclosed arena when the schooling area is outside in bright daylight. Under these circumstances, the first fence should not be a rustic brush but, rather, a white board brush box that is clearly discernible. Similarly, a fence should not be located in a darkly shadowed or comparatively dimly lit spot. If an obstacle must be placed in a poorly lit area, then it should be lighter in color with a well-defined top line. A grass-topped gray wall, for example, would not be the proper choice in this case. The position of the sun during early morning or late afternoon during outdoor show sessions will also adversely affect the horse's performance. If jumping classes are scheduled during low sun periods, every effort should be made to avoid forcing the competitor to jump directly into the sunshine. This is one of many good reasons why show management should schedule under-saddle classes at the end of the afternoon sessions.

In addition to lighting, color intensity may occasionally startle a horse. Large items, such as board coops painted stark white, seem to cause more refusals than those painted in earth tones or simulated stone motifs. According to Moyra Williams in *Horse Psychology*, the horse's eye receives a powerful stimulation from massive white objects that in turn excites the brain and results in an agitated horse. Identical background and obstacle colors often blend and render the top of the obstacle indiscernible. A white gate in front of a solid white background will be difficult to jump no matter how well the course designer defines the ground line.

Finally, the fence decorations themselves may cause a horse to balk. Artificial and real flowers are routine embellishments in today's hunter courses and some horses simply have not had enough exposure to overcome their fear of these unfamiliar objects. Knowing this, the prudent designer will use less elaborate decor on a novice course than on a classic course. Classics may be quite colorful and adorned with banks of flowers surrounding the wings. Hunter fences, however, should not be numbered and flagged because these objects would be quite unfamiliar to the hunter and are not at present required by the rules.

Modern hunter courses are far more sophisticated than a few post and rail fences in a field. A hunter course designer must consider the size of the arenas and topography of the land. He or she must know how to artfully utilize the fence inventory and when to adjust the jumps to compensate for poor footing or lighting. Most important, the designer should understand the galloping stride and arc in flight of both horses and ponies. Building hunter courses is the responsibility of a qualified designer who has made the effort to research and learn the craft.

A final word to the exhibitor. Riders should note that as the quality of hunter competition improves and the sport of horse showing endeavors to attract more spectators, horse show courses will consist of the longer-stride distances and more colorful obstacles. As mentioned earlier in this section, most courses for open hunter sections and classics are designed to accommodate the 13-foot stride and today's show horse should be able to negotiate these distances effortlessly. It is also fair to "expect" that hunter courses will include flower boxes, water troughs, pillared wings, artificial logs, and so on. A hunter should be properly introduced to these obstacles, or a near facsimile, while training at home or in schooling shows.

Many books have been written about training and showing horses. I will not attempt to deal with that subject in detail inasmuch as this book is about designing fences and courses. But, in preparing for the show ring, the rider should school his horse over a variety of cavaletti and gymnastic combinations to improve the horse's form, balance, and cadence. Jumping defects can be corrected by simple exercises: trotting square oxers to improve the arc; jumping vertical and horizontal cross-poles to prevent drifting; and using offset poles to sharpen a dull, inattentive horse. A variety of distances can be used between fences in a combination to force the horse to lengthen or shorten his stride and/or arc, and experimenting with these distances and types of obstacles to suit the stride and jumping of a particular horse will bring the best results.

In addition to jumping in the proper form, the show hunter should also execute smooth flying changes of lead and negotiate the turns in a proper balance, without "cutting in" or "bulging out" of the line of the curve. Depending on the lay of the land and the sequence of obstacles, it may be necessary to lengthen or shorten the horse's stride between fences. It is interesting to note that a horse's stride can be compressed to as short as 8 feet at the collected canter and lengthened up to 28 feet at racing speed. The possible range of variation is 20 feet! Adjusting the horse's stride is an exercise that should be practiced at home, so that either alteration can be performed smoothly without disturbing the horse's attitude. If the fundamentals are learned at home, the horse should have few unexpected difficulties with the show course. Simple discipline results in winning hunter performances.

Courses for
Three-Day Events

BILL THOMSON

Bill Thomson.   Bill Thomson is a veterinary surgeon as well as one of the leading three-day event and horse trials course designers in the world. A resident of Little Bytham, in England, he has been one of the major cross-country course designers in Great Britain for the past two decades. As a technical adviser to the British Horse Society, he has had a hand in the design and construction of dozens of courses for all levels of competition throughout the United Kingdom, and he has also designed courses in the United States and Canada.

Mr. Thomson has been responsible for the course at the Burghley Horse Trials, one of the two principal three-day events in England, for more than a decade, and he has been responsible for the design and construction of six European and two World Championship three-day courses. His book, *Constructing Cross-Country Obstacles,* is an acknowledged classic on the subject. As Major D. S. Allhusen says in the foreword of that book, "There is no one better qualified to write a book on the subject of the construction of cross-country obstacles in Horse Trials than Bill Thomson."

The Background of the Three-Day Event

I suppose that at one time or another the majority of people who own or ride horses have attempted to make a fence of some sort in an effort to encourage their mount to jump. As often as not such fences are totally inadequate, for their flimsy construction only encourages carelessness and, when they collapse, they leave the horse alarmed and slightly puzzled and probably determined to take no further risks.

I, too, indulged in this sort of pastime with my childhood ponies, but for very many years now I have made a great number of fences for other people to jump in a lot of different competitions, both at home and abroad, and I believe, through the painful experience of trial and error, I have in many cases at last arrived at the quickest and simplest method of constructing really lasting obstacles. These, I hope, may be of value to others when faced with the problems of course designing and fence making.

To my way of thinking, artificial fences fall into four different categories — arena, steeplechase, cross-country, and schooling. In this book I am concerned with the last three types. Arena jumps and course setting are highly specialized subjects and differ from their cross-country counterparts as chalk does from cheese. (In Chapter 1 Pamela Carruthers, one of the world's greatest experts on arena jumping courses, explains the complexities that her expertise has mastered.)

Steeplechase fences are a subject apart. There are several ways of making them but the end product, in Britain at any rate, should always look much the same, so a section in this chapter is devoted to the various ways of constructing them.

Cross-country fences may be fixed and solid or of the knock-down type. The scope and variety of the latter are apt to be rather limited but,

even so, some of the designers of modern hunter trial courses are constructing them with an ingenuity that was unthought of a few years ago.
However, it is to the fixed and solid fences that I owe my allegiance, for
their construction frequently calls for improvisation and imagination.
There is always a different problem to be solved and a new line of
thought to be pursued, and the finished article is just as neat and tidy
as your skill can make it.

Schooling fences belong to any one of the four categories, and their
object, primarily, may be to teach a horse to jump but, latterly, to enable
horse and rider to practice over the type of obstacles they expect to
meet in competition or in the hunting field. In order to simulate the
many different types of fences that exist, schooling fences should be
adjustable for height. Yet it is helpful if they can be fixed and solid,
should the occasion demand it. They may be the least interesting fences
to make but no one can deny their importance, for it is on adequate
schooling that competitive success depends.

Before in any way considering the methods of planning and constructing cross-country courses, it is essential fully to understand the background in which the courses are planned and the standard of severity or
simplicity at which they are set.

The story stretches back for many years, for presumably fences have
been jumped ever since horses have been ridden. It is not until comparatively recently, however, that the horse has ceased to be the main
means of transport and has largely assumed the role it plays in sports-
manship and entertainment.

It is really only in the outbacks of the world that the horse is still an
integral part of the pattern of everyday life; elsewhere he has become an
athlete and, as an athlete, a specialist. A very high percentage of horses
are bred for a single purpose. The racehorse is the obvious example.
He is bred for the flat or to race over fences. His heritage may endow
him with the splendid speed of the sprinter or the stamina to stay in the
race. In their own way, too, the trotting horse, the Hackney, the polo
pony, and many others have their future prenatally destined, and this is
how it has to be, for in the standard of competition, as it exists today,
only the best can hope to achieve any sort of success. It is, however, a
system that has one great drawback, for many of those who fail to make
the grade in their own sport are often diverted to some other branch of
equestrianism for which they are unsuited and in which they last no time
at all. In Britain, as in Ireland, this last contingency was really of no
account, for there has always been a big and steady demand for genuine
hunters from whom a good deal of versatility was required and whose
experience in looking after themselves in the hunting field gave them a

wisdom that enabled their owners to enter them for hunter trials, steeple-chases, and even arena jumping competitions. But this was not the case in Europe. Hunting there was not the traditional country sport and was only enjoyed by comparatively few, so that the demand for the more versatile horses was largely limited to military uses. As early as the beginning of this century, this type of horse was no longer in abundance and, in an effort to encourage the breeding of such horses, various com-petitions were devised. Their objects were, to quote the *Cavalry Journal* of 1906: "To promote the practical training of the warhorse for long distance and cross-country work, and in a thorough schooling and handi-ness, and to arrive at the best type of horse and the best way of condi-tioning and handling him."

As these competitions were the immediate precursors to the modern three-day event, it is perhaps worth considering, briefly, the conditions under which they were held. They were called International Long Dis-tance Competitions and that of 1906 took place on three different days at two-day intervals. All starters carried 165 pounds — which is the weight carried by all competitors in the modern three-day event — and, on the first day, the horse was ridden some 26 miles in a set time. This distance included nine fences in the middle section of the course and nine in the last section. The pace required over the jumping sections was 400 meters per minute but, as the distance of these sections is im-possible to ascertain, the speed required in the intervening sections is not known. In the second stage of the competition the horse and rider had to complete 31 miles in 4 hours and then, after a rest of 2 hours — and an inconceivably unpeaceful rest it must have been — a steeple-chase course of about 2 miles was ridden at 600 meters per minute. The length of time, too, has persisted to this day for the steeple-chase phase in the endurance test of the modern three-day event. In the third stage horses had to negotiate a jumping course that tested their handiness which, presumably, involved several sharp turns and changes of rein. A form of dressage test was ridden prior to the start of the competition.

By 1912 this competition had been modified until it much more closely resembled the competition as we know it today and, for the first time, it was included in the curriculum of the Olympic Games, that year held in Stockholm. From then until the beginning of World War II, participation was confined almost entirely to the military. In 1948, when the Olympic Games resumed, they were held in Britain. Organizing an Olympic three-day event is always a gigantic task but, on this occasion, it was made much more difficult by the fact that the records of the 1936 Berlin Games were not available. However, after many vicissitudes of fortune, both to competitors and organizers, the event was concluded. The United States competitors were the worthy winners; Great Britain failed to finish as a team. This was a great disappointment to the British riders, for there is no doubt that competitors from the host nation have a considerable advantage — environmental and psychological — both to themselves and, even more so, to their horses. Britain's defeat in these Games could be regarded as the root cause of the renaissance of combined training in this country; although "renaissance" is scarcely the word, for the sport was so little known that few were even aware of its existence. I believe this new enthusiasm radiating from Britain has done a great deal to stimulate eventing in North America and on a worldwide basis. This is how it happened.

After the 1948 Olympic Games, the Duke of Beaufort, much impressed by this competition, which he had witnessed for the first time, and, one might guess, much depressed by the fact that the British riders had been unable to acquit themselves more successfully, offered the use of Badminton Park to the British Horse Society so that they might organize a national three-day event there. This they did. The event held in April 1949 was a great success, and it has been organized there nearly every year since. Its original intention was, of course, to encourage more riders to compete, so that Britain would have a greater field of experience from which to select a team for the 1952 Helsinki Games. To this end it succeeded beyond the wildest expectations for, not only did it open the sport to many more civilians, but it stimulated a number of imaginative people in different parts of the country to hold much smaller events. These events last for one day only and originally provided a splendid schooling ground for the three-day event. Nowadays these one-day trials have become a sport in themselves and provide a great deal of pleasure to very many riders who have little aspiration to seek international honors. I have described the background to modern eventing in Britain in some detail, for I believe it is a pattern that has been repeated in many countries throughout the world.

The Federation Equestre Internationale (FEI), based in Brussels, is the governing body that dictates the conditions under which all international three-day events are conducted. Anyone who hopes to become a cross-country course designer must, therefore, be fully conversant with their rules and with the modifications worked out in their own country, laying down the conditions under which their smaller national events are conducted.

Not only is it essential to know the rules but also the aim of any given competition and exactly what it hopes to achieve. International three-day events fall into two categories; the Concours Complet International (CCI), which is a competition in which individuals compete, and the

Concours Complet International Officiel (CCIO), which is both an individual and team competition.

The third category is, of course, Concours Complet d'Equitation Olympique, which is essentially a team competition, but there is also a concurrent individual classification.

I am sure that by far the majority of readers of this book will be conversant with the structure of the modern three-day event but, for those who are not, I will briefly describe it.

On the first day the dressage test is ridden. The test is issued by the FEI or a national federation for national events, and its purpose is to prove the rider's method of training and his horsemanship, as well as the horse's suppleness and obedience. On the second day the same horse and rider have to take on a course of up to 20 miles, which, broadly speaking, involves some 13 miles of roads and tracks, 2¼ miles of steeplechase course, and 4½ miles of cross-country course with up to thirty fixed and solid fences. In this test, the rider shows his ability to ride at all paces over all manner of obstacles, to save his horse where he can and yet get the maximum performance from him. The horse must prove his boldness, wisdom, and stamina. The last test, which takes place on the third day, is the arena jumping. It is designed to prove the horse's fitness, willingness, and ability to remain in service after the tremendous effort of the previous day. It will be seen, therefore, that the primary aim of a three-day event is to prove the versatility of both horse and rider. The four phases that comprise the endurance test start with Phase A, which is a section on the flat that has to be ridden at a fastish trot or slow canter, or a mixture of the two. Phase B is a steeplechase course with up to ten fences which is, obviously, a galloping section. Another phase of roads and tracks precedes the cross-country course, which must be ridden at a pretty smart gallop both between and over the fences.

The maximum and minimum lengths of the various phases are as follows:

For the CCI, phases A and C (roads and tracks), a total of 10 kilometers to 16 kilometers must be carried out at a speed of 240 meters per minute. In phase B (steeplechase), 2880 meters to 3450 meters are to be carried out at a speed of from 640 to 690 meters per minute. For phase D (cross-country), from 5200 meters to 7410 meters must be carried out at a speed of from 520 to 570 meters per minute.

For the CCIO and Olympic Games, phases A and C take a total of 16 to 20 kilometers, at a speed of 240 meters per minute. In phase B, 3450, 3795, or 4140 meters must be covered at a speed of 690 meters per minute. For phase D, 7410, 7695, or 7980 meters should be ridden at a speed of 570 meters per minute.

These are the distances and speeds printed in the FEI Rule Book and I regret that I must go into some detail to explain their significance. For timing phases A and C, the chosen distance divided by the chosen speed (240 meters per minute) gives the optimum time. Finishing either of these phases in a faster time than the optimum time gains nothing, but exceeding the optimum time leads to one penalty mark for each second up to the time limit, which is 20 percent more than the optimum time.

In phases B and D the optimum time is similarly calculated as for phases A and C. A competitor is penalized .8 of a penalty point, in the case of phase B, and .4 of a penalty point in the case of phase D for each second in excess of the optimum time up to the time limit, which in the case of phase B is twice the optimum time and in phase D corresponds to a speed of 225 meters per minute. Exceeding the time limit involves elimination.

The variations in the choice of speeds and distances in the different competitions enable the course designer to complement his fences and control the degree of difficulty of the course and the overall severity of the event, not just by the fences alone. Whatever distances and speeds are chosen, they must be the most suitable for the standard of the entry that is expected and for its quality and state of preparation.

In order to ease the task of preparing the timetable and that of the timekeepers, the distances and (in the case of events other than CCIOs) speeds chosen must give an optimum time to a whole minute or a whole minute and thirty seconds. This is achieved automatically in the CCIO because the speeds are constant, and the distances are also constant. The distances for phase B are 3450, 3795, or 4140 meters. In phase D they are 7410, 7695, or 7980 meters and none other. But it is not so in a CCI or other national event, for with a choice of speeds there is no constant factor. The length of the courses must be in multiples of half the chosen speed, falling between, in phase B, 2880 and 3450 meters and, in phase D, 5200 and 7410 meters.

There are several other factors that have a very considerable bearing on the broad outline of course designing. The first of these is, perhaps, a consideration of the relative influence of the different tests on the final result of any competition conducted under the FEI rules.

Tests must not be confused with phases; the tests are dressage, endurance, and arena jumping. The phases are the four sections that comprise the endurance test. The FEI states that, in principle, the relative importance and influence on the final classification should be in the ratio of 3 dressage, 12 endurance, and 1 arena jumping and that the course and conditions of the competition should be arranged to conform as closely as practicable to this ratio. This sounds like a well-nigh impossible ratio to set out to achieve, and whether it is achieved or not cannot be ascertained until the competition is completed. A complicated mathematical calculation is required for each competitor's score, setting up a standard deviation that will reveal the ratio of the three tests as created by those competitors who finish the competition. However, it is seldom, if ever, that all competitors do finish, and those who do not have no score and, therefore, no influence on the final ratio. But, in fact, if they were eliminated for refusals on the cross-country course, they have exerted a greater influence on the final ratio than most of those who complete the course. In order to obtain a reasonably accurate result, these eliminated competitors must be allocated some score, and many people have different ideas as to what it should be. Probably the best solution is to give them the score of the lowest placed competitor.

In order to facilitate, or even make possible, the course designer's task of making a course that exerted approximately the right influence on the competition, the FEI introduced a multiplying factor that is applied to the dressage marks. The dressage tests for CCIs and CCIOs are infrequently changed and, therefore, before the introduction of the multiplying factor, they exerted a pretty constant influence in every competition. In order to attain the correct ratio, the course designer had to realize that it was the standard of the dressage that dictated the severity, or otherwise, of the cross-country course and, indeed, the arena jumping. Now, however, by the use of the multiplying factor, the influence exerted by the dressage may be increased or reduced. The factor may be between .5 and 1.5 but none other. The good marks each competitor scores in the dressage test are averaged (there being three judges), subtracted from the maximum marks obtainable, and then multiplied by the chosen factor. If the low figure is employed, the spread between the marks of each competitor will be reduced, and the influence exerted by this test will be correspondingly lowered. If the higher factor is used, the reverse will be the case. Under this system the course designer is given a great deal more latitude; he can vary the severity of his courses a great deal more and still approximately achieve the correct ratio. If the course is rated as severe, the high factor will be used to match the influence of the dressage to the trouble that is anticipated on the cross-country course. If, on the other hand, it is fairly simple, then the low factor will be taken. It is the technical delegate who assesses the dressage factor. He does it after he has seen all the phases of the course, knows the standard of the entry, and has appreciated the weather conditions and the going. The latter may well alter, for the factor is announced immediately before the dressage starts, but, with the endurance test only 24 or perhaps 48 hours away, he should have a pretty strong indication as to what conditions will prevail.

It must also be remembered that, in order to keep the arena jumping in line with the other two tests, the lower the multiplying factor that is imposed, the more simple — or perhaps it would be better to say the less severe — the jumping course must be.

First Design Decisions

This seems to be a long preamble before getting down to the meat and bones of course design and fence construction, but I have learned, as have many others, that time spent on reconnaissance, both mental and physical, is never wasted. A course designer must know exactly what he is hoping to do and the reason why. Once the conditions laid down by the FEI for the conduct of international events are fully understood, its motive becomes apparent, and the modifications of national rules governing lesser events take on a sharper outline. For instance, no national federation would ever think of laying down a definitive relative influence of tests for one-day trials but they all probably suggest that the influence exerted by the dressage test should be slightly more than that exerted by the arena jumping test but considerably less than that exerted by the cross-country one.

There are more FEI stipulations which international course makers must observe when considering the design of an international course. In few instances they can apply to national one- or two-day trials but, nevertheless, their implication should be followed as a guideline.

In an international event, the number of obstacles in phase B — the steeplechase course — should number three to every 1000 meters and in phase D — the cross-country — four to every 1000 meters. These figures do not scale down well for national events for, proportionately, there would be far too few fences. Under these conditions, a 2-mile course would only include fourteen fences. Thus the national federations have set forth rules governing the number of fences for such competitions. Latterly, some course designers have been skirting the rules by including a number of obstacles of several elements that bear only one number but may cause the horse to leave the ground two or three times to negotiate them.

There are, in fact, two types of multiple obstacles that will be met on most cross-country courses. In one type, each part of the fence is considered as a separate obstacle and is numbered and judged independently. Thus a competitor may refuse twice at each part of such a fence without incurring elimination and he may not re-jump any part. In the second type, the obstacle has several elements, all bearing the same number, with an alphabetical suffix — 1a, 1b, 1c, and so forth — which is judged as one fence. The original reason for this type of obstacle was to enable a competitor to extricate himself from a fence where the elements were so close together that, after a refusal at the second or subsequent parts, there was insufficient room to re-present his horse without retaking an element or elements that he had already jumped. Recently, their employment has been extended to include obstacles such as banks, ramps, steps, or ditch and rails that are designed as one complete test. With the limitation to the total number of obstacles allowed for any given length of course, there was a great temptation to include quite a number of these fences. This rather defeats the object of this rule for, in this way, several courses, in the opinion of the FEI at any rate, were including too many actual leaps. To control the course designer the FEI, in the latest edition to its rules, states that "the number of obstacles composed of several elements may not exceed a ratio of one in ten over the whole course."

I will not here state in detail the maximum heights and spreads for the various standards of international courses, nor would it be possible to do so nationally, for they vary considerably from country to country. The point I do wish to make is that only 50 percent of the total number of obstacles in an international course may be of the maximum height and that the last obstacle on the course must be not more than 150 meters and not less that 50 meters from the finish. These, again, are international rules but they give very good advice to the course maker, whatever grade of course he is making.

I think the maximum heights and spreads mean very little; it is the standard that counts. Do not mistake me, they must be observed. If a 1.10-meter (3-foot-7-inch) maximum height course is required, it is obviously a pretty novice course that is wanted. Although a very great deal depends on the terrain, it is unlikely that there will be any call for even 50 percent of maximum obstacles, unless, perhaps, a lot of flat ground has to be utilized. Flat ground and good going call for a maximum effort. Equally, in a one-day trial, the position of the last fence may be dictated by a natural fence line or some other expediency. It must, however, be far enough away from the finish to give the timekeepers long enough to identify the riders as they finish but close enough to preclude a long wild gallop. Often it is not so much the position of the last fence that decides the distance, but the siting of the finish which, as I will explain, goes hand in hand with the start.

During my career with the British Horse Society, I have been closely concerned, if not totally responsible, for producing the courses for five CCIOs, over twenty CCIs, and literally hundreds of national events throughout Great Britain. When designing courses, the procedure adopted is very much the same for a novice (preliminary) one-day trial as it is for a CCIO; the difference is in the magnitude of the task. Never can courses be made solely for horses; there are far too many other contingencies to be considered, and they must be considered and sorted out long before any sort of detailed planning of the cross-country courses takes place. If combined training is going to grow and expand, it must be a financially viable sport, with a considerable degree of control exercised from a central office. The work that this involves increases with the numbers of competitors that yearly join the ranks of combined training. Membership and subscriptions may possibly pay for office and staff maintenance but they certainly do not pay for the organization of events. Therefore, events have to pay their way, certainly in the long run, and once they have become established they should be able to show a profit.

I think many of us in Britain find it hard to appreciate the problems faced by the United States Combined Training Association and by American competitors. Britain is a small country, and there are a large number of trials in a comparatively small area. Distances traveled in order to attend events are infinitesimal and a great deal less costly than in the United States but, even so, if competitors were asked to pay for every aspect of their sport, I doubt if it would last a season. Thus, the people who help to pay for the trials must be the watching public and, in order to attract them, they must be given every facility. This must always be kept in mind, particularly during the initial inspection of a new site.

Assume that an estate owner has applied to hold a CCI and has asked for advice on the general layout of the event and the courses in particular. The first step is, of course, to go and have a look on the widest possible basis to ascertain whether or not the site is feasible. Until recently, no one would consider offering land on which to run an international horse trials unless they were pretty interested and knowledgeable about all the various facets of combined training. Thus the chances were that the few sites offered would be feasible. Nowadays, in Britain anyway, this is no longer the case, for there are a number of big parks that are not put to intensive agricultural use, and the trend is to convert them to pleasure centers where permanent facilities for a number of different sports, including horse trials, will be available to the public. Under these circumstances, it is more than possible that the owner of the proffered land has no equestrian background whatsoever. These circumstances make a course designer's task a good deal more difficult, for he will have to find out everything for himself whereas, with a knowledgeable owner, a great deal that is useful would be shown to him.

Before even looking at the site it is essential to know what scale of event is considered. Is it to be one of some magnitude, encouraging as many members of the paying public to attend as possible and providing them with every sort of facility, or is it to be run more cheaply in a much less ambitious way? Perhaps these considerations would appear to have no bearing on the design of the cross-country courses, but indeed they do. The more spectators, the bigger the car parks, the greater need for tentage, the more the social services, the larger the jumping and dressage arenas, and so on. All these amenities, which in a big event are as important as the courses themselves, must be planned in conjunction with them. Frequently, indeed, they must be given priority, for seldom is there a flat enough area on which to construct the arenas in the most convenient place. The first consideration should be the suitability of the access and egress roads and, if a big event is envisaged, these must be good and there must be several of them. Seldom is an event site adjacent to a freeway, which means that traffic will have to be filtered through secondary roads before even reaching the ground. This, in itself, can be a major problem and should be referred to the local traffic authority before any decision is finalized.

The next step is to decide the position of the arenas. There may be little choice, according to the conformation of the terrain, but, if there is, they should be so positioned that there will be sufficient room for parking between them and the access points and also for the social amenities around their perimeter, as well as a fairly large collecting ring. A free area of ground must be available in close proximity for warming up on the dressage days. As the arenas will be the social hub of the event, pleasant surroundings do a lot to create a good atmosphere.

The General Survey

It is now possible to decide the general direction of the cross-country course (phase D) and the best situation for the steeplechase course (phase B). The latter must be on reasonably flat ground with level and good going. From the point of view of both expense and convenience, it will probably be a two-circuit course, with half the required number of fences, each of which will be jumped twice. Even so, it is surprising what a large area of ground it will occupy. On the Continent there is a very different concept of a three-day event steeplechase course: they are often laid out in a figure of eight or even more complicated patterns, so that the track crosses in two or three places. My own opinion is that there is more than enough to worry about during the endurance test of a three-day event without running the risk of a collision on the steeplechase course, although I must admit that I have never heard of such a thing happening. The position of the steeplechase course may be at a considerable distance from the start of the cross-country course; indeed, if necessary, as far away as the total length of phase A but, from the spectators' point of view and those who are assisting competitors, it is much more convenient if it is reasonably close to the remainder of the event.

Having settled the position of the steeplechase course, a detailed survey is made of the land over which the cross-country course is going to be laid out. The start and the finish must be in the same place, but may be in the same or opposite directions; whichever is chosen, the course will be a closed circuit. During this survey, there are a number of other observations to be made, as well as seeking out the more interesting places on which to construct fences. Frequently this inspection is made during the winter, whereas the event will probably take place in the summer. I have already discussed the importance of catering to the public, and one of the things it appreciates is being able to see two or three fences without moving from one place. In winter it is very difficult to appreciate the extent of summer's foliage and how much it limits visibility, but it must be taken into account. The going must also be examined, and any false ground or wet places will be marked on the map which, of course, is an essential at this stage and should be of a large scale. Equally, interesting features and natural fence lines should be marked on it. With this more detailed examination must go consideration of communications and both vehicle and pedestrian access to all parts of the course.

Once all these considerations have been studied and the map marked up with all the information that has been gleaned, it is possible to link up the noted fences on it and draw out a continuous course. The course may take a roughly circular track or it may loop round various features in an irregular manner. The latter is the more interesting; indeed, if the outward leg can come quite close to the inward, the grouping of fences for spectator viewing is greatly facilitated. Whatever type of course is adopted, as far as possible the changes of rein should be wide and sweeping between the fences.

It may be impossible to include all the interesting places and bold features that were discovered. The question is to decide which to incorporate and which to discard. It is never worth spoiling the fluency of a course in order to reach one particular area of ground. It is very easy to develop a preconceived idea as to which way the course should go, clockwise or anticlockwise. Some of the features discovered will undoubtedly present a more interesting problem if jumped in one direction rather than the other, and it is only by balancing up the pros and cons of these situations that decision may be taken.

Once the proposed track of the course has been established, it must be measured to insure that its length is within the maximum and minimum allowable. Before setting forth with a measuring wheel, it is as well to get a rough idea from the map. Should the distance from these measurements be short or excessive, the knowledge of the ground gained from previous reconnaissance will make it very much easier to decide where a loop must be added or a corner shortened. There is a small instrument manufactured for measuring distances on a map and it is quite accurate if the map is of a fairly large scale. It consists of a small wheel mounted on the end of a handle on which there is a dial that registers how far the wheel has been pushed along. I admit to finding them not altogether satisfactory — their road-holding propensities are poor and they are apt to skid on corners! I prefer using a length of string, which can be pretty accurately laid along the track of the course, then measured back on the scale of the map.

Measuring on a map takes no account of hills and, on very steep terrain, the distance measured on the ground will probably be slightly longer than that measured on the map. The map measurement must be confirmed by measuring on the ground. The instrument that accomplishes this works on a similar principle to the map measurer. The wheel is from 1 foot to 18 inches in diameter, depending on the make, and the dial will count in either yards or meters. Some of these instruments are fitted with pneumatic wheels while, in others, the wheel is solid. It is important, in the former type, that the tire should be kept at the recommended pressure for, obviously, altering the circumference of the wheel impairs the accuracy of its measurements.

When measuring the course on the ground for the first time, it is wise to measure along the track of the course from one landmark to the next, noting the distance between each. Better still is to drive pegs into the ground at given intervals — say, every 300 meters. If, when the measurement is completed, the course is found to be either too long or too short, it is possible to add or to remove a given distance without having to remeasure the whole thing. For instance, a course is planned to be 4560 meters long. When it is measured, it is found to be 4405 meters. Therefore, 155 meters must be added to bring it up to the correct length. A suitable place to do this may be between the fourth and sixth peg — a distance of 600 meters. Thus, measuring from the fourth peg, an extra loop will have to be incorporated, measuring a total of 755 meters before joining up with the original measurement at peg six. By this means, a great deal of work may be saved for, although the wheel is easy to push when the going is good, it can be very heavy in wet ground or long grass and it must be very seldom that a good course is the right length at the first attempt.

It is possible, although ill advised, to push the wheel while sitting on the fender of a jeep or Land Rover that is driven by a companion. If the going is smooth, measurements taken in this way will be quite accurate but, on rough going, it is impossible to prevent the wheel from jumping and spinning while in the air. I doubt if any cross-country course is flat enough for this method to be relied upon. There is also a further hazard to the jeep way of doing things. If a speed of more than four miles per hour is attained, the wheel is very difficult to steer. If it hits a tussock of grass, it is liable to twist round in the hand and dart quickly beneath the automobile, which is dangerous for both the wheel and its

Fig. 1.   A Typical Novice One-Day Trial Layout

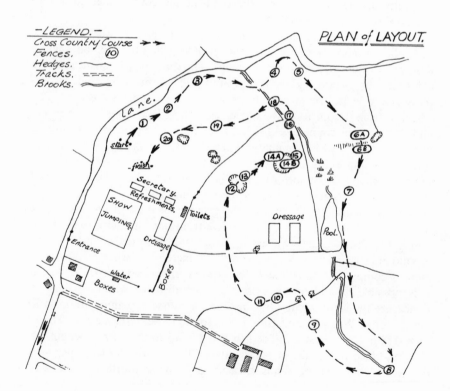

operator, for his reaction is to cry out in immediate dismay. In helpful response the driver, who cannot see the wheel anyway, crams on the brakes — which may save the wheel but not the operator. He, now controlled by the irresistible forces of inertia, has no option but to leave his perch on the fender and describe a neat parabola to land face downward on mother earth!

Figure 1 shows a typical layout for a novice or preliminary horse trial. It illustrates all the points I have been discussing that the course designer and builder must take into consideration. All competitors must be given such a plan before the course walking, and such a plan should be included in the program prepared for the spectators.

Where to Start and Finish

With the course now fixed at the correct length and including all the features that have been decided upon, the time has come to fix the position of the start and the finish. It may seem that this should have been done as soon as planning started. No doubt some idea of its approximate position will have been formulated during the exploratory period, but its exact position depends on a number of considerations. I will describe the start and finish area in some detail, for the whole success of the event depends on efficient scoring and time-keeping.

A well-designed start and finish area (Figure 2) facilitates both these difficult jobs. The area will include the start of phase A, the finish of phase C, and the start and the finish of phase D. In it there must be room for the timekeepers, the veterinary inspection panel, a doctor and a first-aid tent, a veterinary surgeon (not connected with the inspection panel), and a farrier. There must also be a weighing tent and, in many events, the scoring tent is in the vicinity as well. In all, it will occupy an area of about 50 meters square, with a pulling-up area of about 100 meters after the finish of phase D, and it must be laid out on level ground. As the first two or three fences on the cross-country course should be pretty straightforward, in order to allow horses to settle into their stride before meeting the more hazardous obstacles, it should be situated some distance from the first of the more exciting features.

Another factor to be considered is the situation of the stables. It is obviously more convenient if it is laid out on the same side of the circuit as the stables, so that competitors have access to it without the need to get through the general mêlée of spectators and car parks.

In order fully to understand the implications of the design of any given start and finish area, it is necessary to have some knowledge of the

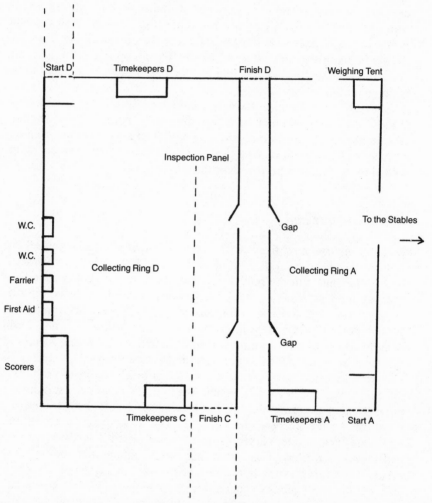

Fig. 2.   A Well-Designed Start and Finish Area

problems of time-keeping in a three-day event. Prior to the start of the endurance test, each competitor is issued with a timetable that gives his starting time for each phase, based on the optimum time. If the demanded times for the phases are: phase A, 20 minutes; phase B, 5 minutes; phase C, 40 minutes; phase D, 11 minutes, a competitor's timetable would read: Start A at (say) 11.00 hours; Start B, 11.20 hours; Start C, 11.25 hours; Finish C, 12.05 hours; Start D, 12.15 hours. There is a compulsory 10-minute pause between finishing phase C and starting phase D. During this time the inspection panel decides whether or not horses are fit to continue after completing both phases of roads and tracks and the steeplechase course.

If a competitor fails to complete phase B in 5 minutes — say he is very slow and can get round no faster than 6 minutes 7 seconds — the rest of his timetable is thrown out of gear. At whatever time he finishes B, he is still allowed the full optimum time to complete phase C, and the 10-minute pause is sacrosanct. Thus, his correct finishing time for C will be 12.06 and 7 seconds and his starting time for D, 12.16 and 7 seconds. Similarly, if he is faster than the optimum time on phase B, his finishing time for C will also be advanced that much. However, his starting time for phase D will remain as fixed by the timetable and he will, therefore, have a slightly longer rest than the compulsory 10-minute pause. Perhaps I should have mentioned that the finishing time of B is always the starting time of C, for competitors finishing the steeplechase go straight on into phase C without hesitation.

The intervals at which competitors start is a decision entirely to be taken by the organizers of any individual trial. My advice for a three-day event is that 4 minutes is the best time. Five minutes is a boringly long time for spectators; 3 minutes gives headquarters a worryingly short period in which to get things under control if something goes wrong, such as a bad fall or a smashed fence.

There is also a collecting ring at the start of the steeplechase course, which houses the timekeepers for the finish of phase A, the start and finish of phase B, and the start of C, which, again, I would impress, are synonymous. However, this is a very much more simple setup and will logically follow the design of the main start and finish area.

Because the start and finish of phases A and C are widely separated, the only method of timing them is by time of day. This is done by the use of split-second chronometers, which are very accurate watches with two full sweep second hands that run concurrently until the operator presses the knob on the top of the watch, whereupon one of the second hands stops and he is then able to read off the time of day to the nearest second. There will be five or six of them stationed at: Start phase A;

Finish phase A; Start phase B. The same watch may also time the finish of phase B, or another one may be used, and either of them automatically record the starting time for phase C; Finish of phase C; Start and Finish of phase D. The watches at the start of phases B and D send off competitors according to their timetable or its adjustment. The scorers receive the times of day that were recorded at the various starts and finishes and, from them, are able to deduce the elapsed time taken by each competitor for each phase.

In addition to the chronometers, the two highly important fast phases — B and D — are also timed with stopwatches or any other device that records elapsed time. It is obviously a cross check and it is thoroughly necessary, for amateur timekeepers may read a watch wrong — which is much easier to do than anyone who has not tried would possibly believe. First, it is generally pretty easy to decide which is the correct time. Second, it is not unknown for a watch to break down, and, third, even very expensive chronometers can lose or gain 7 or 8 seconds in the course of 6 hours.

Looking at the design of the start and the finish area depicted in Figure 2, the reason for the siting of the start of A is obvious; it has uninterrupted access to the stables and, subsidiary to that, the track of A is outside the cross-country circuit and probably will not have to cross it in order to reach the start of the steeplechase course. Phase C finishes straight into the collecting ring of D and, as each competitor finishes, he moves along a roped-off lane directly to the inspection panel. After being passed by them, he spends the remainder of his 10-minute halt in this collecting ring before moving up to the start of phase D. It is very helpful for the inspection panel if the members can see each horse coming toward them over the last 300 or 400 meters of phase C, for it helps them to appraise his condition and the advisability of allowing him to continue.

The starts of both A and D are formed by a pen 5 meters square, and the latter is in line with the finish and the timekeepers are situated on that line. It might be thought, therefore, that it would be easy to time D with one chronometer, but there is a countdown for each competitor at the start of D that can only be done from a chronometer and, during this time, another competitor might finish.

Whether or not the scorers should be situated in the collecting ring D or completely divorced from the start and finish area is a matter of opinion but, if they are divorced from it, they must have quick and reliable communications to the starter of phase D. They and they alone can implement the rule concerning the independence of various phases and inform the starter of adjusted starting times. It must be remembered that no adjustment can be made until each competitor has completed phase C, for it is possible, although unlikely, that someone miscalculates and takes longer than the optimum time on that phase. I favor the idea of the scorers being on the spot, so to speak, so that there is immediate and personal communication with the starter. The scorers, if sited in collecting ring D, should be placed out of the way and on the side of the collecting ring that is within the circuit of the course, so that the collectors of the jump judges' scoresheets may reach them with the minimum delay and without the hazards and difficulties of crossing the track of phase D.

After finishing phase D, competitors pull up and, without dismounting, return to collecting ring A. There, under the eye of the weighing steward, they climb onto the scales to insure that they make their 75 kilograms (165 pounds) before returning to the stables and a well-earned rest.

If it is more convenient for the general layout to have the start and the finish of phase D in opposite directions, very little modification to the plan is needed. The finish of phase D would remain in the same place but the direction arrow is reversed. The start of phase A and the timekeepers would ideally change places with the weighing tent. Phase A would then be starting in the opposite direction to that depicted in the plan. If it were required for A to start in the same direction as on the plan, the timekeepers would have to be moved to the other side to allow room for competitors to get to the weighing tent after pulling up. The tent would be situated between the two gaps.

The width of the run-in would be about 6 meters. Just how this whole area is to be fenced in depends entirely on the number of competitors and how many spectators are expected — and a surprising number of them will congregate here at the start of the endurance phase. Under pressure, the only safe way of fencing it is with some sort of paling (chestnut paling or snow fencing) along the long sides, with stakes roped together on the two short sides, with suitable gaps. The run-in should be paled on both sides, with two gaps in the suggested position. It is worth bringing the paling back at the gaps, as illustrated, so that a horse finishing does not actually see them and has no tendency to hang toward the other horses in the collecting ring.

There is some merit in arranging the start and the finish in opposite directions, for adjusting the length of the course is made a good deal easier. Obviously, moving their position by, say, 100 meters adds on or removes a total of 200 meters.

Roads and Tracks

The conditions governing the length of phases A and C — the roads and tracks — have already been stated and, by and large, the route that they will take will be dictated by the country in which the trials are being held. If, however, there is any choice, there are a number of factors worth considering.

First, the time of year must be taken into account, so that the type of weather expected may be anticipated. If it is expected to be very hot, without humidity, woodland trails should be chosen — partly because they are likely to be cooler and partly because such trails are almost certain to have better going. If the humidity is high, open country is preferable.

Paved roads are permissible but are much better avoided. As long as the trails are wide enough for horses safely to pass each other, it does not matter if both phases use the same trails, with horses going in opposite directions. I would say, in fact, this is often something that is much appreciated by competitors. Phase C, particularly, is a long and lonely ride with a big build-up of apprehension as the competitor nears the start of the cross-country course. Under these circumstances, to pass another rider and have a word with him helps enormously to ease the tension.

It will almost certainly be necessary to set up boundary markers (red or white flags) to prevent competitors from taking short cuts. All red flags must be placed on the rider's right and all white flags on the left. However, there is little object in putting up flags and hoping that competitors will meekly obey their message if there is no one in a position to check that they do. This is a dreadfully boring job to do but, if the roads and tracks go in opposite directions along the same trail, one person is able to watch two flags, and often the direction from which a competitor approaches is a strong enough indication that he went the right or wrong side of a previous marker.

The Steeplechase Course

In planning the steeplechase course, the initial reconnaissance is to find a sufficiently large area of reasonably level ground. The inclusion of inclines, as long as they are not too steep, is perfectly acceptable. Indeed, they probably favor the more skillful riders whose experience will tell them when to save their horses and when to send them on.

Once the site is found, the proposed course must be measured. This is rather more difficult than measuring a cross-country course. There will probably be no landmarks to make it possible to take an initial measurement with any degree of accuracy from a map. However, the ground will be level, and that means smooth rather than without undulations. It should, therefore, be possible to take the first measurements from a vehicle.

The course is likely to be a rough oval, which will be half the total distance, so that two laps with five fences — each jumped twice — will constitute the phase. Some like to have a change of rein included, which may be achieved by "denting" one of the long sides of the oval. If the first measurements are taken from a vehicle when the grass is wet from rain or dew, the wheels of the vehicle will leave a mark which will last for several hours and is extremely useful inasmuch as it is possible to see exactly what line was taken on the first measurement without having to drive in pegs. Make the turn at one end of the oval near the edge of the available site, so that there is room to expand it should the initial measurement be too short. When the first nearly accurate measurement has been achieved, the two sides and the one end of the oval should be marked out with pegs. The distance between all the pegs is measured, then it is perfectly simple to discover how far the other end of the oval must be extended or contracted to attain exactly the required distance.

Once again the start and the finish must be close together, preferably in a straight line. The finish of phase A must be in close proximity. The finishing point of phase B is automatically the starting point of phase C. The start and finish area (Figure 3) should be sited on one of the long sides, for there must be a good straight run to the first fence and it should continue for at least 100 meters before coming to the first turn. It is likely that the finish of phase A and the start of the second roads and tracks, together with their direction, will indicate the most convenient situation for them and also whether the course will be ridden as a left-hand or a right-hand circuit.

Figure 3 is a drawing of a typical layout for a steeplechase collecting ring. Horses will remain in this collecting ring only for a very few minutes, for no one wishes to hurry unduly on phase A. Therefore, it does not occupy a very large area. A 25-meter square is perfectly sufficient.

In order to segregate the horse that is about to start from the one that is completing the first circuit and commencing the second, a run-in to the main course from the collecting ring is more than advisable. If the starting interval is 4 minutes, it is most unlikely that a horse would

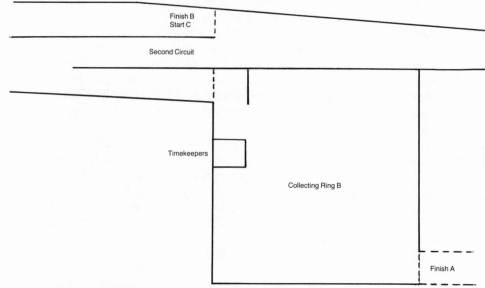

Fig. 3.   Start and Finish for Steeplechase

be finishing the first circuit at the same moment as another was due to start but, should such a situation arise, the starter must use his discretion and delay the start. Under the most exceptional circumstances it is possible for two horses to arrive at the junction of the run-in with the main course at the same time but, to guard against such a contingency, it is safer to have the run-in to the main course on the inside of the circuit. To do this means that phase A will have to cross the steeplechase course. The crossing place should be arranged so that it is on a narrow front, and maybe it is worth putting up a notice that states "Phase B. Look Left [or Right]." It must be made plain to competitors that, where phases cross, the faster phase has the right of way.

As on the cross-country and roads and tracks, red or white boundary markers will have to be erected on all the turns, to prevent riders from cutting the corners. These should be large and made more obvious by placing a hurdle or some straw bales at their base. It is much more pleasant riding round a turn at the gallop if it is continuously defined by stakes and rope or string. However, this is time-consuming and expensive, as well as being unessential. But, if no string or rope is used, the boundary markers should be within 30 or 40 meters of each other.

In Europe the fences on the steeplechase courses are really a smaller edition of the cross-country fences — post and rails, log piles, triple bars, and so on. In Britain all the fences on the steeplechase course are made out of birch and are quite uniform in their appearance, save one or two may include ditches. In the United States and Canada the steeplechase fences follow the design used in Britain but, instead of being packed with birch, spruce or some other evergreen material is used.

Before describing in detail the method of constructing steeplechase fences of this nature, it is worth considering the general principle of their number, positioning, and dimensional limitations as laid down by the FEI.

They state that, on average, there should be three fences to every 1000 meters. This means that, from the shortest permissible CCI course to the longest CCIO course, their number will vary from nine to twelve. It is more satisfactory if they are fairly evenly spaced throughout the length of the course.

I will not quote the maximum heights and spreads for the various types of fences in the different competitions but I will quote what I think is the all-important rule that limits every category of international steeplechase fence for three-day trials. "In both the competitions [CCI and CCIO] the fixed and solid part of steeplechase obstacles will not exceed 1 meter [3 feet 3 inches]. Brush fences will not exceed a height of 1.40 meters [4 feet 7 inches]." This means that the European type of fence may not exceed 1 meter, yet in a CCIO the spread of a ditch in front of, say, a post and rails of that height may be as wide as 3 meters (9 feet 10 inches), which presents a pretty uncompromising sort of obstacle. Let us shut our eyes to this type of obstacle and take a closer look at brush fences, be they made of birch or spruce.

Steeplechase Fences

There are two basic ways of making brush fences. The first is to construct them actually on the site so that, once made, they remain in position until they are destroyed. The second, and obviously the more economical, way is to prefabricate them in movable frames, which can be set up in position a short time before the trials and then dismantled soon after and stored under cover, away from the eroding influence of the weather.

Figure 4 depicts the type of fence that is made on site. Such fences, as already stated, may be as high at 1.40 meters (4 feet 7 inches) but probably they will be 5 centimeters (2 inches) lower than that. The base, measured from the front of the take-off board to a point immediately below the overhang at the top of the fence, will be about 1.70 meters (5 feet 8 inches). As only one horse at a time will be jumping

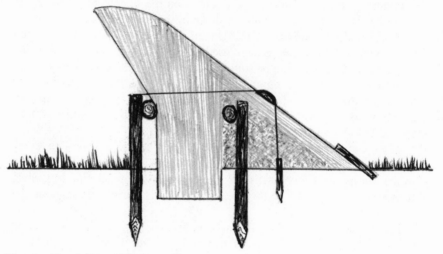

Fig. 4.   Brush Fence Made on Site

these fences, they need be no wider than 5.49 meters (18 feet), exclusive of wings.

To construct such a fence, dig a trench at right angles to the line of the course, 5.49 meters long, 0.30 to 0.54 meters (1 foot to 18 inches) wide, and 0.30 meters (1 foot) deep. Along both sides of the trench drive posts into the ground at 1.37-meter (4-foot-6-inch) intervals, keeping them as near to the edge of the ditch as possible. To the inside of these posts, and about 0.61 meters (2 feet) above ground level, nail rails to each row. To reduce the risk of splitting the wood, leave the posts slightly longer than 0.61 meters and cut them off flush after the rails have been fixed in position, and blunt the nails before driving them. Now block up one end of the frame with two crosspieces.

Whatever material is to be used, it is much easier to handle if it is tied into bundles. If birch is to be used, I would say each bundle should contain about 24 saplings. Spruce is a great deal more bulky and half that number should be sufficient. Each bundle must be tied two or three times throughout its length, so that it more resembles a cylinder than a bunch of flowers. To fill the frame of a fence of these dimensions will take about 75 bundles but, obviously, it is difficult to be dogmatic, for everything depends on the size of the bundles! The object is to stuff as many bundles into the frame as possible, so that the finished result is a pretty hard and unyielding obstacle. The bundles should be about 2.13 meters (7 feet) long and the finer the better.

Fig. 5. Compressing Bundles in Brush Fence

There are many ways of compressing the bundles in the frame but the method described now is a satisfactory way of doing it and requires very little in the way of equipment. Insert eight or nine bundles into the frame at the blocked-up end, with their butts in the trench. Now pass a rope round these bundles inside the frame and just below the rails. Fasten both ends of the rope to the front of a tractor or jeep and reverse slowly away, while an assistant with a heavy hammer or bar encourages the butts to move along the trench as the bundles compress. When they have compressed sufficiently, tie another rope around them and the end of the frame, to prevent them from springing back once the tension is relaxed (Figure 5). It is only by trial and error that the height at which the rope is held round the bundles may be ascertained. If it is too high, the tips of the bundles will be pulled over more than the butts, and vice versa. This must be rectified immediately, for once the bundles take on any degree of slope, the fault becomes quickly exaggerated.

This process is repeated until the frame has been filled. Each time more bundles are compressed, the holding rope is undone and retied around them. The last few bundles will have to be rammed in by hand before the open end of the frame is closed.

A formidable obstacle has now been produced, which must be clipped down to whatever height is required. The hard way to do it is by hand, with long-handled secateurs, but, if it is possible to get hold of an efficient mechanical hedge trimmer, an immense amount of time and really hard work will be saved. Whatever tool is used, it is important that, when the top is clipped, it is of a uniform height throughout its length. If a post is driven into the ground on each corner of the fence, then a length of string may be attached to these posts and stretched tautly around the fence at the height at which it is to be clipped. The top of the finished fence will slope upward from front to back, as will be seen from Figures 4 and 6. The string, although not an infallible guide to a level clip, is, nevertheless, a great help.

Having completed the framed part of the fence, it is now possible to add the apron, which gives it its attractive rake and helpful ground line. Again referring to the diagram and the previously stated dimensions, it is easy to accurately position the take-off board, which should be 0.30 meters (1 foot) wide and 0.037 meters (1½ inches) thick and of the same overall length as the fence. It should be set into the ground 0.075 meters (3 inches), firmly pegged into position and angled so that it conforms to the slope of the apron. The space between the take-off board and the frame is filled with spruce, or what have you, laid horizontally and then faced with individual saplings laid vertically, with their butts firmly wedged behind the board.

A rail, known as the guardrail, is now laid across the vertically positioned saplings, in order to pull them into the frame of the fence and consolidate the whole apron. This guardrail should not be more than about 0.61 meters (2 feet) above ground level. It is quite a tricky job fixing this rail at exactly the right height and, at the same time, to put sufficient pressure on it to really consolidate the apron. If it is just wired straight through the frame to the back rail of the fence, whenever any tension is put on the wires, the rail tends to roll up the slope of the apron. To prevent this from happening, four or five pegs are driven firmly into the ground immediately below the line of the guardrail. Wires are stapled to them and passed over the guardrail and through the fence. The wires may then be tensioned, either with a wire strainer or by attaching them, one at a time, to a vehicle. While the wires are being strained, it is a great help to have assistants to hold the rail in position.

It is now possible to clip the vertically placed saplings, so that they merge into the top of the material in the frame. The take-off board and the guardrail should be painted an orange color, with a mat paint, so that they can never be shiny.

Wings must be added to the fence to provide a degree of obscuration at either side. On a racecourse, wings are angled toward the take-off side and are at least 3.658 meters (12 feet) long. In horse trials the length of wings is a matter of opinion. Indeed, the majority of 'chase fences that I have made have been provided with wings that are a

Fig. 6.   Completed Brush Fence

straight extension of the fence. It is quite a good idea to leave the last few bundles of filling in the frame unclipped (Figure 6). They give a blended appearance to the wings. The wings will be made from a wooden framework, which is threaded with filling material that should be at least 1.825 meters (6 feet) long.

The prefabricated type of fence is made in very much the same way, save that a rather different type of frame replaces the trench and the rustic posts and rails are replaced by sawn timber. Each fench (Figure 7) will be made up of two frames, each 2.74 meters (9 feet) long, 0.71 meters (2 feet 4 inches) high, and 0.45 meters (1 foot 6 inches) wide.

Fig. 7.   Frame for Prefabricated Brush Fence

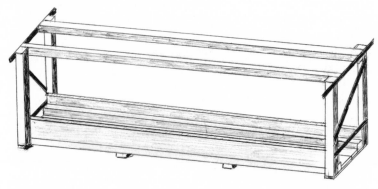

These frames will be made out of 0.1 by 0.075 meters (5 inches by 4 inches) sawn rails, and all the fixings should be made with 0.0123-meter (⅜-inch) coach bolts.

First, the front and the back of the frame should be made. These are then joined together at a width of 0.45 meters (1 foot 6 inches) with three iron bars: one situated near the top of the two sides of the frame, one near the bottom, and one diagonally from top to bottom. The top bar should be wider than the frame by 0.05 meters (2 inches) on both sides. There should be a board, some 0.15 meters (6 inches) wide, fixed to the inner aspect at the bottom of both the front and back side of the frame. The bottom of the frame is then boarded over, so that, together with the two planks, an artificial trench is formed.

Packing them with whatever filling material is preferred is done in exactly the same way as for a fence made on site. It is probably easier to do if the frame is first fixed down to the ground. This is done by putting two frames together, end to end; a squared knot-free post is driven into the ground at each corner and where the two frames join. The protruding iron bars are then bolted to them. It is necessary to use iron bars to join the ends, for they need to be only 0.0082 meters (¼ inch) thick, so that the ends of the frames fit together without any appreciable gap. A horse jumping a fence of this nature, without the company of others, will also go over the middle. It is, therefore, important that the frames are made accurately, so that either end may be joined to either end, thus potentially doubling the life of each frame. The apron and wings are applied to these fences in exactly the same way as previously described.

An open ditch (Figure 8) requires a slightly different technique. The frame is made in the same way, whichever type of fence used. The ditch is then dug out, and a take-off guardrail is fixed in position. In a CCI, the maximum spread, measured from the take-off side of the guardrail to a point immediately below the furthest point of the overhang of the packing material, must not exceed 2.80 meters (9 feet 2 inches) or, for a CCIO, 3 meters (9 feet 10 inches).

The take-off rail may be made out of railway ties, telegraph poles, or any other substantial timber. It should be around 0.375 meters (1 foot 3 inches) high and should be let into the ground about 0.10 meters (4 inches), so that there is no possible chance of a refusing horse sliding into it and catching a hoof beneath it. The fence will, in the main, be jumped better if it is painted in a light orange color with mat paint. There will be no apron as such, but the frame will be covered by a screen of packing material, and a guardrail will be pulled to hold it there.

Some people recommend that, in the case of an open ditch, the guard-

Fig. 8.   Brush Fence with Ditch

rail should be concealed, so that horses approaching the ditch do not see two parallel rails — the take-off guardrail and the frame guardrail. In the open ditch (Figure 8), it will be seen that the frame guardrail is not only exposed but also painted the same color as the take-off guardrail. Maybe it would be wiser to creosote it but I would not obscure the highest solid part of any fence with flimsy material, although I would agree that any horse that hits the frame guardrail is bound to fall, whether he sees it or not.

The ditch will be about 0.61 meters (2 feet) deep and a tremendous illusion of height is created if the butts of the packing material are taken right down into the bottom of the ditch — indeed, if they are let into the soil there, the apron is a lot easier to fix. On the walk round before the event takes place, the competitor's eye is carried, with no break, from the top of the fence to the bottom of the ditch — a height of some 2 meters (6 feet 6 inches) — and it gives the appearance of a very big fence indeed! It is an illusion that is entirely wasted on the rider mounted, or on the horse, but it is impressive to spectators.

There is, in Ireland, a company that is manufacturing plastic birch fences. They have been in experimental use at one or two racecourses in Ireland, Britain, and the United States, and one was used at the

Fig. 9.   Two Views of a Plastic Birch Fence

CCI, held in Britain in 1973. Although not everyone in the racecourse fraternity finds them fully acceptable, the expense of making and maintaining the sort of fences described is becoming so prohibitive that the use of the substitutes may become virtually obligatory. They consist of a metal frame, the back of which is just under 1 meter (3 feet 3 inches) high and it is joined to the front part, which is much lower, by a stepped platform. Each step of the platform is drilled through its length with 0.012-meter (½-inch) holes, 0.05 meters (2 inches) apart. Individual sprigs of plastic foliage of about 0.61 meters (2 feet) are inserted into each hole. The stalks of the sprigs terminate with a collar and about 0.025 meters (1 inch) of thread, to which a nut is applied in order to hold the sprig in position (Figure 9). The apron is made from molded foam rubber, which is held in position by very strong green canvas on which simulated take-off and frame guardrails are painted with mat orange paint. Wings are added in the normal way.

They do not look too bad from a distance but, on closer inspection, they appear exactly what they are — completely artificial. It is the top rail of the back of the frame that makes them unpopular on the racecourse where, in Britain at any rate, our birch fences have no fixed and solid part higher than 0.61 meters (2 feet). It conforms to the FEI rules and, although heavily padded with foam rubber, it is totally concealed and totally unyielding and, if a horse really stands off and comes down onto the top of the fence, it seems that he would be bound to hurt himself.

The Cross-Country Fences

So much for the steeplechase and the roads and tracks. The fences on the cross-country course, which are really what the course is all about, fall into the two categories of artificial or natural. Under the heading of natural I would consider such things as paddock railings, stone walls, banks, and so on, but, before describing any sort of cross-country fence in any detail, there are one or two rules governing their construction which should be constantly borne in mind.

I quote Article 337 of the FEI Rule Book: "Cross-country obstacles at which a horse in falling is likely to be trapped or to injure itself may only be built in such a way that part of the obstacle can be quickly dismantled and can be quickly rebuilt exactly as before. Such a construction must not in any way detract from the solidity of the obstacle." And again: "The obstacles must be fixed, imposing in shape and appearance and left, as far as possible, in their natural state. Artificial obstacles must not constitute an acrobatic feat of jumping for the horse, nor be designed or intended to give unpleasant or unfair surprise to competitors. In no case, one single bar which would give the horse the opportunity of passing underneath, may form an obstacle." What it really amounts to is that everything possible should be done to insure that a horse making a bad mistake does himself the minimum damage.

Fences are surrounded by a penalty zone. The penalty zone is a rectangle, extending 10 meters (11 yards) before and 20 meters (22 yards) beyond the obstacle, to a width of 10 meters (11 yards) on each side of the boundary flags marking the limits of the obstacle. Falls and disobediences are penalized only when they occur within this zone. This zone may appear to be of no great concern to the course constructor, but a sequel to this rule states that entering or leaving the zone without having jumped the obstacles to be negotiated is penalized as a refusal. This sequel makes the rule of very considerable interest and, as will be seen later, it plays an important part in the design of multiple obstacles.

To go back to natural cross-country obstacles. It is very seldom that any fence is ever found in its natural state that does not need some kind of modification. A well-made cross-country course should insure that all the fences present exactly the same silhouette at the end of a competition, as they had at the beginning. With natural fences this would be very difficult to guarantee. Natural fences are usually jumped in the middle, so that something like a hedge takes all the punishment in one place. Such a fence must, therefore, be artificially thickened and strengthened, which may be done by stuffing packing material into it. If this method is adopted, spare material must be left by the fence and the fence judge be instructed to make good any damage, immediately it occurs. It must be done at once, or there is risk of a catastrophic breakdown.

Hedges may also be protected by fixing a rail in front of them or above them, but never in them or behind them. I would repeat, never must a solid part of a fence be concealed by flimsy material (Figure 10). A single rail, fixed in front of a fence and at about the same height as the top of it, forms a thoroughly false ground line, which encourages the horse to get too close to the fence before taking off. Obviously enough, the ground line of a fence is where it touches the ground or comes close to it. If the ground line is immediately beneath the highest part of the jump, it is said to be a true ground line. If the lowest part is brought forward to the take-off side of the fence, as in the steeplechase fences we have just examined, it is said to be a helpful ground line, but if the reverse is the case, such as a single rail in front of a hedge, or perhaps even a wall, the ground line is said to be false (Figure 11). Jumping a fence of this nature, at speed, is a pretty chancy business.

A paddock gate, I suppose, could be called a natural fence. It would be a straight-up obstacle with a true ground line. Unless especially constructed, it would be smashed to pieces if hit hard by a galloping horse.

Fig. 10.   Never conceal solid part of fence by flimsy material.

Fig. 11. *Top,* True Ground Line; *middle,* Helpful Ground Line; *bottom,* False Ground Line

The weakest part of it is right in the center, and that is exactly where every horse will jump it. It will be fastened to a gatepost at both extremities and, rather than reinforcing the highest part of it — which makes it look top-heavy anyway — dig in a third post behind the middle of it, which is cut off flush with the top rail. When a gate is broken, it usually ends up in fairly small pieces. To avoid the anxieties that will accompany the ensuing holdup, it is well worthwhile making sure that it is certain to remain intact throughout the whole competition.

Natural walls also form a straight-up true ground-line type of obstacle but the coping stones, whatever they are made of, are abrasive and unyielding, and must be protected by some means or another (Figure 12).

Fig. 12.   Railway Tie Protects Top of Natural Wall.

Removing them and replacing them with railway ties is one way of dealing with them. Cementing a quadrant-sectioned rail to the take-off edge
forms an adequate protection. Whatever sort of shield is used, fixing it
immovably in position always presents a problem. It is one that is never
insoluble with the application of a bit of ingenuity. What is hard is to
blend the shielding material to the wall, because the ambition always
is to keep the wall looking as natural as possible.

It is not often that a wall can be found to include in a course. They
are expensive to build; if one is found in the right position but is too
high for the standard of the competition, do not despair. It is always
much less expensive to build up the ground on the take-off side than to
knock off the top and have to rebuild it at a later date. However, a word
of warning! If the ground is to be made up, it is quite possible to do so
with binding gravel just a short time before the event but, if soil is used,
it must be put down at least six months to a year before the course is
ridden, and grassed over to insure that it is thoroughly consolidated.
If gravel is put down on grass, it produces a sudden color contrast, and
if it is not spread a good way back from the fence, a horse might be
encouraged to take off from the edge of the gravel and far too soon. I
well remember riding in a steeplechase in England many years ago.
There was a fence situated in a nicely harrowed plowed field. The
landowner had thoughtfully left about 6.10 meters (20 feet) of unturned
grass in front of it. Mine was a very bold horse who was always inclined
to make his own arrangements, and he decided that that was exactly the
spot from which he would take off. He landed smack on top of the fence.
I think it was the only time in my life that I have actually stood on the
pommel of my saddle! However, I did get back in again without hitting
the deck, but it was a rather painful process.

The majority of artificial cross-country fences are basically formed out of post and rails. Whatever type of timber is used for constructing them must be really substantial. Flimsy-looking materials encourage careless jumping. Indeed, rails that look to be quite thin but are, in fact, very strong are extremely dangerous.

The height of finished fences will, of course, vary according to the standard of the competition for which any given course is being made. The maximum and minimum vary from Training Level at 1 meter (3 feet 3 inches) to the Olympic Games at 1.50 meters (3 feet 11 inches). Eight inches does not seem a very wide variation from the best to the worst but, in certain circumstances, an inch or two can make all the difference in the world. Posts and rails may be bolted or wired together but they must finish up at the exactly intended height. Frequently it is not the standard of the competition but rather the configuration of the ground that dictates the height of fences, and it is not always easy for the course builder to get these heights dead right. However, it is a great help if some sort of prop (Figure 13) is designed, in order that top rails

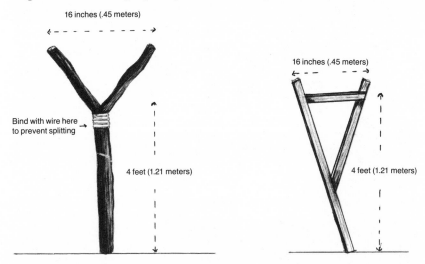

Fig. 13.   Props to Help Position Top Rails

can be firmly held in position without fixing them, so that their height may be adjusted. It is impossible, when constructing fences on broken ground, to specify what height they shall be until they have been seen in position. They can be raised or lowered on the props until the course constructor's eye tells him he has got them in the right position. This is an attribute that some people have got almost instinctively; others may pick it up from experience, either from riding across country themselves or by looking at a lot of courses with clinical observation. For me it has always seemed astonishing that some people who have never indulged in any sort of active riding can be first-class course designers. It does not follow at all that first-class riders across country necessarily make good course designers.

It is not possible, in print, to explain how or why difficult and broken terrain is used to produce interesting fences, because the object and design of such obstacles depend entirely on the ground and each must present its own problem, both to the designer and the rider. Figures 14, 15, and 16 show two fences that are well suited to the particular terrain on which they are sited. A horse will not have much idea what he is going to be asked to jump as he approaches either of them. This is,

Fig. 14.   Approach to Well-Sited Fence

Fig. 15.   Same Fence as Figure 14, Showing Detail of Ditch

however, in no way unfair. With the rail in Figure 14, for example, the rider knows exactly what is in store for him and he must use his skill and take command.

Figure 14 is the same fence pictured in Figure 15, as seen from 30 meters (33 yards) in front of it. The first view the horse will get of the ditch is probably one stride out, but the rider must have him balanced and prepared so that there is no problem in negotiating the spread. Figure 16 is a photograph of a step-down, with the ground falling away steeply on the landing side. As this fence is approached, no ground can be seen on the landing side for at least 100 meters (110 yards) and it will not be seen until the very last stride. Once again, it is the rider who must do the thinking.

With drop fences, the FEI does lay down some guidelines, for it is

Fig. 16.   Step-Down Fence

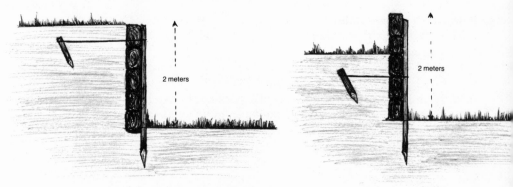

Fig. 17.   Measurement of Drop Fences

very easy to include too many in any given course. It is now a rule that the number of obstacles with a drop of between 1.60 and 2 meters (5 feet 3 inches and 6 feet 6 inches) is limited to two on any course. The total of those with drops of less than 1.60 meters is left to the discretion of the course designer or, in the case of a CCIO, to the technical delegate. If a drop fence is so designed that a horse jumps down onto the flat, the distance of the drop is simple to measure. If the landing is on a downward slope, as in Figure 16, so that the horse continues downhill after landing, the drop is virtually impossible to measure. It entirely depends on how fast or slowly the fence is negotiated. Figure 16 represents a pretty formidable obstacle, and heaven forbid that anyone should jump it at speed, but a smaller version could be jumped from a walk, trot, or canter, and the distance of the drop will depend entirely on the speed of the contestant. Figure 17 illustrates the FEI's intention.

Limitations have also been imposed on aquatic fences. Where horses are asked to jump into or out of water, the depth must not exceed 0.50 meters (1 foot 7½ inches) and that depth must be maintained for at least 5 meters (16 feet 5 inches) on the landing side of an obstacle in the water and for the same distance on the take-off side of a fence out of water. I would stress here that, if horses are to be asked to jump into or out of water, it is absolutely vital that the landing and take-off areas are completely sound and will remain so throughout the competition. My advice would be that, if there is any shade of a doubt, do something about it or relinquish the idea altogether. It is insufficient to tip gravel alone into a soft-bottomed pond or stream. It must be preceded by a thick covering of fairly large stones, gravel is used to fill up the cracks and unevennesses. Obviously some judgment must be used, for if the site is a morass nothing on earth will make it ridable.

A fence built in water, positioned so that the horse jumps out of water and lands in water, must be very firmly fixed and not too high. It is kinder if something in the nature of a post and rails is used, rather than a tree trunk. A horse moving at any speed through water creates quite a big bow wave, which will pass straight through a post and rails but will burst against a log, causing a lot of spray before the horse actually jumps. It is doubtful if it occludes a horse's vision to any great extent, but it does make the rider very wet. From this point of view, too, if there is any choice — which I will admit is seldom — it is far more pleasant for riders if water fences come late in the course. When jumping them, even if all goes well, the rider gets pretty wet and it does nothing for his comfort during the rest of his ride.

In the absence of natural fences in the right place, artificial ones must be constructed. Now that an amendment has lately been published by the FEI, limiting the number of multiple fences to three on any course, many more straightforward big fences will have to be made. Alternative fences, which I will discuss later, are not infrequently an interesting way in dealing with uninteresting ground. Here are a few suggestions for fences in the open on the flat.

Parallel rails, or double rails as I prefer to call them, can be made to look spectacularly big and indeed, when they get to international dimensions, they are. They are much easier to jump and look far less compromising if they are lightly filled with some sort of greenery. But, never must the back rail be hidden. The top rails are held on blocks and lashed down with cord so that the fence may be quickly dismantled, for a horse jumping short at a parallel rails may well become hung up. For this reason, too, there should be no lower rail beneath the farther top rail. Figure 18 shows another way of making a collapsible rail. In this case,

Fig. 18.   Detail of Collapsible Rail

Fig. 19.   Problems with a Parallel Fence (Photo by George F. Barnes.)

Fig. 20.   Two Table Fences

the posts were supporting the second rail of a V-shaped fence which, for various reasons, was impossible to lash. The posts were kept upright by two metal struts that joined the extremities of both rails and were held in position by bolts fitted with wing nuts.

Figure 19 is a photograph of a horse that has taken off far too soon while jumping a big parallel. He has hit the farther rail with his forelegs, tipping his hind legs high into the air. Had he just cleared the farther rail with his forelegs, almost for sure would his hind legs become trapped between the top and lower rail, both of which are fixed.

A table fence is a good safe obstacle and might be regarded as a parallel with the top filled in. Figure 20 shows variations of a table fence; *A* is a sand bunker jumped toward the camera. It had a platform, which was constructed about 0.15 meters (6 inches) down from the top, and the space so formed was filled with gravel. *B* is an imitation saw bench. I think it is worth mentioning that, if any object is to be simulated, it must be really well made or the result is messy and thoroughly amateurish.

The log pile (Figure 21) looks as though it contains an awful lot of timber; however, only the outside layer is rails and they are packed up on logs about 0.61 meters (2 feet) long.

Fig. 21. Log Pile

Fig. 22.   Lamb Creep from Take-Off and Landing Sides

Fig. 23.   Stone-Faced Bank.

The lamb creep (Figure 22) is a gadget not infrequently seen. Its object is to allow lambs to pass between the struts in order to feed while, at the same time, excluding the ewes.

A stone-faced bank, as that depicted in Figure 23, is charming to look at but very expensive to build. Depending on the time of year, it must be made at least six months to a year before it is jumped, in order to allow the turf to become firmly rooted. I would think that this particular bank is too narrow and a lot of horses would fly it. That may have been what was intended, but banks are normally made for horses to jump onto.

Figures 24, 25, 26, and 27 are self-explanatory, save to say that the appearance of a rustic seat (Figure 27) is improved out of all recognition if arm rests are added at either end.

Fig. 24.   Pen Fence Combination with Drop

Fig. 25. Tires Used in Jump

Fig. 26. Slanted Birch Rails

Fig. 27.   Rustic Bench

Ditches, whether natural or dug out for the occasion, usually need some sort of protection to the take-off bank. Few can withstand sixty or seventy horses jumping over them in much the same place without wearing away considerably. It may be done either with a take-off rail, or by revetting with railway ties or some other stout timber. Using a take-off rail is the cheaper and easier method but, if the width of the ditch has to be altered, revetting is the only answer. A take-off rail should be around 0.30 meters (1 foot) in diameter. About one third of its width should be let into the ground on the edge of the bank and it must be immovably fixed in position. Any turf between it and the ditch should be removed. Revetting is a tedious business and entails building a wooden wall to retain the whole depth of the bank. It is always worth-while treating the timber with some preservative and anchoring the supporting uprights back into the bank about 0.45 meters (1 foot 6 inches) below the surface. In this way the work will last for very many years.

Obstacles in Combination and Multiple Obstacles

Obstacles in combination are fences that consist of two or more elements and each is generally considered as a separate fence and is flagged and judged independently. A competitor may, therefore, refuse twice at each element without incurring elimination but he must not, under any circumstances, retake any part of the obstacle that he has already jumped. However, if an obstacle formed of several elements is designed as one complete test (Multiple Obstacle), or the elements are so placed that it is impossible for a competitor to continue from the same point after a refusal, each element is flagged and marked with the same number, but with an alphabetical suffix. In this case, a competitor, after a refusal at the second or subsequent elements, may return and retake the complete fence. Emphasis should be put on the word "may," for that is exactly what it means — he does not have to!

To help to illustrate these rules, Figure 28 shows two fences at right

Fig. 28.   Fences at Right Angles

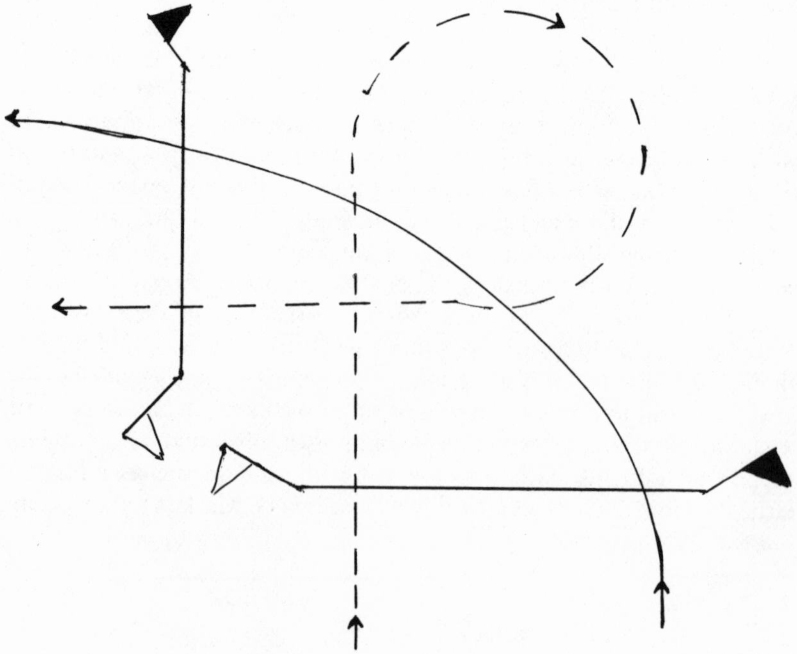

angles to each other. If they were numbered with the same number, plus suffix, the continuous line would be the track to be followed. If they were numbered separately, either the continuous or the dotted line could be taken, if there were not overlapping penalty zones. If the dotted line is followed, the fence judge must be sure that the horse has not entered the penalty zone of the second fence before the circle was completed. Figure 29 shows three steps up, followed by a rail, all being flagged with red and white flags. If all elements were numbered with different numbers, a horse refusing the rail would not be able to re-jump the steps (dotted line). If the elements were numbered with the same number, plus suffix, after a refusal either the dotted or the continuous line could be followed.

Fig. 29. Step Fence

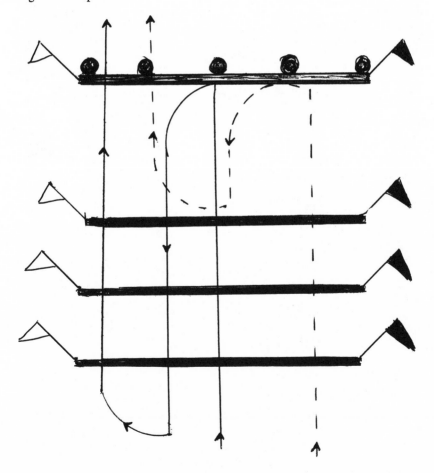

Earlier, the number of fences allowable on the cross-country course was discussed and the rule stating that such fences may only be 10 per cent of the total limits the number of alphabetically suffixed fences to a maximum of three. It is, of course, perfectly possible to include more fences in combination, but each element would have to be independently numbered. Grouping fences so close together would produce a some-what unbalanced course, and there would be long gallops without any fences at all — which is unpopular with spectators and competitors and sets a premium on a fast-galloping horse.

So far, only straightforward multiple fences have been discussed but,

Fig. 30.   Single Alternative Fence

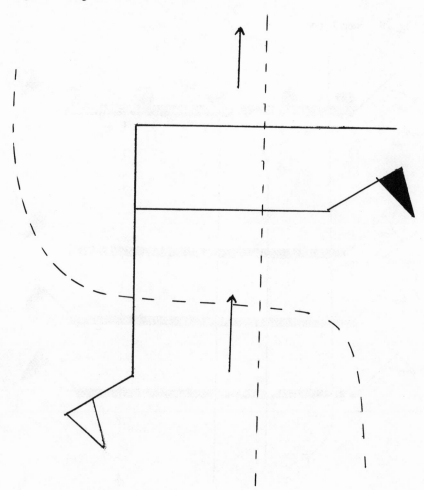

nowadays, many fences are constructed that present a varying degree of hazard, depending on which part of the obstacle is jumped. These are called alternative fences and, generally speaking, the more difficult the part that is jumped, the faster the fence will be negotiated. These fences may be single, multiple, or dependent. Dependent alternative fences are so laid out that the line taken over the first of them dictates where the second and subsequent fences in the complex will be jumped.

Figures 30, 31, and 32 show the plan of a single alternative fence, a multiple alternative, and a dependent alternative respectively. The possible ways of jumping them are marked with dotted lines, and the arrows

Fig. 31. Multiple Alternative Fence

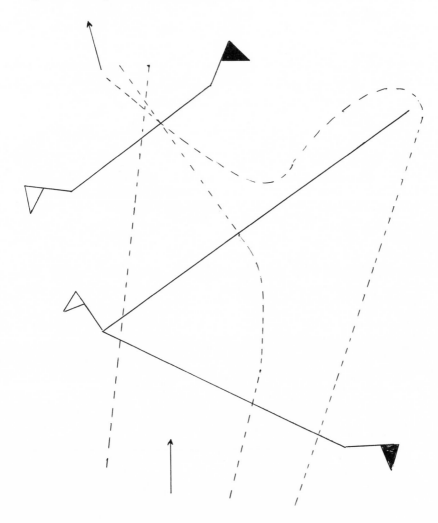

indicate the direction of the course. In each case, the fastest way entails jumping higher obstacles or bigger spreads.

They are fences that require a lot more material and work to construct than the average obstacle. The balance between time and hazard must be very nicely adjusted for, if one part is just too easy, everyone

Fig. 32.   Dependent Alternative Fence

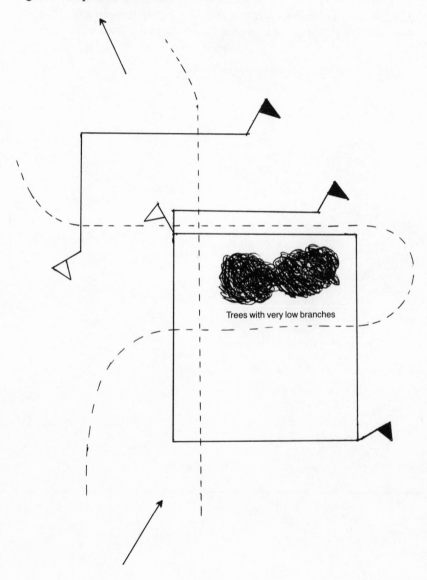

Trees with very low branches

will jump there, and a lot of money will have been spent for no object.

For an individual competition, the balance between difficulty and time may be rather more severe than for a team competition. In the former, the majority of those who still have a chance will generally opt for the quickest route — so long as it is within the bounds of possibility. The saving in time may be as little as 3 or 4 seconds, but multiply that by .4, and 1.6 penalty points may have been avoided.

A team's approach to a cross-country course is rather more cautious than an individual's. It is so much more important for a team to get three, indeed, preferably four, of its members round that unnecessary risks are generally avoided, and the less severe way is usually preferred.

Schooling Fences

It takes a long time and a great deal of talent and patience to bring a young horse up to the standard of performance that is required to compete successfully in events, as they are organized nowadays. Cross-country schooling fences play a very important part in attaining this standard but, not infrequently, individuals' schooling obstacles are woefully inadequate. I am not making any attempt to describe individual fences but, rather, will try to impart some ideas; these, I am afraid, will be valueless if the facilities in the way of land and features are not available.

When making a post and rails, the more uprights it has the better the true ground line and, therefore, the easier to jump. However, schooling fences should be adjustable for height, as well as being solid. If the height is adjusted by raising or lowering the top rail on the uprights, when it is at its lowest, the post tops will be sticking up too high above it. To overcome this difficulty, make up a post and rails at the lowest height required but only make up those parts of it that are aboveground. The uprights may be made out of half-round timber, or any other material, as long as they look substantial. The posts at the extremities are omitted. Prop this up on the required site and put into the ground two strong posts — one at either end — which should be of a height as high as the fence is required to be. Drill these posts at intervals, from the highest to the lowest position, and also drill either end of the rail opposite the holes in the posts. Drive posts exactly behind the uprights of the prefabricated rails and cut them off at the lowest height required at a steep angle, so that no sharp edges are left. When bolted together, it forms an adjustable and solid post and rails, the intervening uprights of which will always be the correct length.

Drop fences are an essential part of the schooling routine. Of course, the falling ground must be available. When jumping such fences, horses are very apt to drag their hind legs. A young horse hitting a solid rail too often may become reluctant to jump. If the fence is made from motor car tires, laid together to form a pipe, no discomfort or injury will result from knocking it. Motor car tires come in all sizes, and old ones cost nothing. If a drop is available, several fences should be made on it, with different degrees of slope and height. It is not a bad idea to make one long fence with three or four sections, each of which is made out of different-sized tires. When suitably prepared, the young horse is first asked to jump the lowest section; as his proficiency increases, he faces up to the next section, which will be a little higher, and so on. The idea is to familiarize him to the obstacle and then kid him to jump a little higher while still jumping the same fence.

Exactly the same principle may be applied to ditches. Be they dug out or natural, they may be enlarged or narrowed by revetting, which all schooling ditches need anyway. A ditch with a front of some 20 meters (22 yards) could be as narrow as 1 meter (3 feet 3 inches) at one end and diverge throughout its length to, say, 3 meters (9 feet 10 inches).

This principle applies even more so to banks. When I was in Ireland in 1973, I stayed with Major Eddie Boylan, one of their top international three-day event riders. He farms and is lucky to have a lot of schooling facilities and the machinery to undertake quite major earthworks. He had constructed a wood-faced bank. Although I did not measure it, I would think it was about 1.30 meters (3 feet 7 inches) high and, from one extremity to the other, some 9.14 meters (10 yards) wide. It measured across the top 2.74 meters (9 feet) at one end and then broadened to 4.57 meters (15 feet) at the other. It had adjustable rails on all four sides, so that it could be jumped in about eight different ways. These rails could also be taken away altogether. Over it a young horse could be taught, first, how to jump onto and off a bank with a stride on top or with no stride on top; second, with a little bit of wisdom to cope with awkward distances; and, third, how to meet a rail off a bank at all sorts of different distances, involving a "bounce" or one or two strides. It also enabled a rider to find out at what speed any horse could find his best stride over any similar sort of fence that he might meet in competition.

Nowadays, when jumping into water has become commonplace, it is absolutely essential to condition a young horse to this type of obstacle. Few are lucky enough to own the facilities to do so on their home ground, but some venue must be found where practice is available. In this context, the fact that all young horses jump so much better at home than they do elsewhere makes jumping other people's fences a vital part of any schooling program.

To my way of thinking, no horse should be entered for any sort of competition unless he is sufficiently schooled to acquit himself in a reasonable sort of manner, even at Training Level. The thoughtless ones who do only cut up the ground for the others, damage the fences, and cause endless headaches to the organization.

I have given you the basic principles to follow both in designing a course and in constructing the obstacles on the course. It is a time-consuming task and requires a good deal of planning. You should not attempt to design and build a course until you have carefully walked and studied courses designed by experienced designers. Only through experience can you get the feel needed to make your course a good one.

A Final Note
from the Editor

ALL THE EXPERTS in this book have set forth in detail the principles, specifications, and sound practices that apply in their specialties. And it goes without saying that course designers and builders must always refer to the rule book to insure that their courses will conform to the current regulations. There are, however, some general principles that apply to all four competitive areas: points that are well understood, of long standing, and not likely to be changed. The purpose of this section is to give the reader a convenient summation of general principles and practices to bear in mind regardless of whether he is going to design and build courses for jumpers, equitation, hunters, or eventing.

First, the good show jumping or eventing course, ideally speaking, is one in which faults are evenly distributed among all the obstacles (except the first one or two, which should prove simpler than the rest), and one which produces a reasonable percentage of clean rounds. The result in a good hunter equitation course is a reasonable number of smooth-flowing pleasant rounds. If no horse or rider can negotiate the course successfully, the designer has set too severe a test for the caliber of the horses and riders competing, or he has designed a course that is unfair in some way. On the other hand, if in a jumper class too many horses go clean the first round and an exhausting series of jump-offs is required, or if in the case of hunters, equitation, and eventing there have been too many good rounds so that the course has not been a very meaningful part of the competition, then the designer has equally failed.

The designer must have a clear understanding of the purpose of the competition for which he is designing the course or courses. For instance, he must evaluate whether the competition is a major one, a championship, or primarily a schooling one. If the designer is not personally familiar with the caliber of the horses and riders he will be testing by his course, he should consult the show management or others who can advise him on what to expect.

The good designer needs the judgment that comes from experience and a feel for the problems a horse is likely to have and the effort demanded of him when faced with a certain situation. Knowing the rules and having a good tape measure are not sufficient. This is especially true of the designer of outside courses at shows and of eventing cross-country courses where terrain can be a major factor in determining if a particular obstacle is an easy or a difficult one.

It is important to remember that a good obstacle, in the ring or out of it, should be strong, heavy, and impressive in appearance. Hunter and eventing obstacles in particular should look natural to the area where they are built. In no case should an obstacle present an unpleasant surprise to the competitor or be an unfair test of the horse. While it is desirable for aesthetic reasons to have show jumping and equitation obstacles that are bright and cheerful, care must be taken not to overdo the use of color or to create a psychedelic extravaganza. Above all, every effort should be made to create a course with many types of fences presenting a variety of tests for the horse and rider.

Good obstacles should be made as wide as possible, bearing in mind that the greater the height of an obstacle, the greater the width should be. As a guide, fences in the show ring should be at least 12 feet wide, not counting the wings or standards holding the elements of the fence. For major show jumping competitions, 15 feet is desirable. Outside course fences for hunters and cross-country obstacles should have a face of at least 20 feet unless clearly framed by well-constructed wings.

When building a set of obstacles for horse show purposes, it is advisable to make all the fittings of a standard size, so that they are readily interchangeable. Walls, gates, Toronto banks, and other filler material designed to fit under rails should be made at least 6 inches narrower than the rails, in order to fit under them without difficulty. It is desirable to make such items in sections so that they may be more easily moved about and stored.

The standards or uprights that hold the elements and poles of an obstacle must be strong and heavy at the base. Some experienced builders make the base of their standards of oak for strength, with the post and other uprights of cedar, which is lighter in weight. Thus the total weight of the standard will not be too great and can be moved easily. The holes in the standards must be absolutely uniform in size and placement, so that the poles will lie straight across at equal intervals and all standards may be used interchangeably. It is best if the interval between holes is no more than 3 inches and if the lowest holes are no more than 6 inches from the ground. It is desirable to have standards of different heights, ranging from 3 feet to 6 feet, but the average standard in a set of jumps should be about 5 feet 3 inches in height. Wing standards at least 30 inches in width are the best for show purposes. They make possible a base that does not interfere with the placing of filler material under the pole or poles and also gives a good frame to an obstacle.

Poles for show obstacles should be from 4 to 6 inches in diameter. Many builders make them of cedar so that they are not too heavy, but some designers, especially of major competitions, like a heavier pole that will not knock down too easily. The more solid-looking the pole the better the obstacle is. Cups have become standard for holding poles and are required for certain kinds of competitions. The metal ones are best, as are metal pins to hold them. Cups should correspond in size to the standards and poles used. For 4-inch poles, a good cup must be 1 inch deep and 5 inches across. Larger poles obviously require larger cups. Current rules state that the maximum depth of the cup must not exceed one half the diameter of the pole. Gates and panels that are suspended from cups must be hung no more than 4 inches from the top and should be placed in cups less deep than those used for poles.

The builder of cross-country courses should use building materials found in the area to give an obstacle a more natural appearance, and remember that different kinds of material help to create variety. There is nothing duller than a course made entirely of telephone poles. Birch makes an attractive fence but does not last very long, and pine also deteriorates quickly. Obstacles in which a horse might be trapped should be built to be quickly dismantled and quickly rebuilt to keep the time schedule of the competition moving.

A good plan of the course should be as detailed as possible, and it is desirable where artistic talent is available to include a sketch of each fence. Dimensions of height and width of all obstacles must be given, as well as the distance between fences in combination, and the plan should clearly show the direction in which each obstacle is to be jumped. As has been pointed out by Pamela Carruthers, if a show jumping competition includes one or more jump-offs, the original course should be designed so that it can be easily converted into the jump-off course. And it is important that the designer keep in mind what he will use as substitute material for a fence that is broken if exact duplicate material is not available.

Definitions

A *vertical* or *straight obstacle,* whatever its construction, is one where all the elements are vertical, one above the other, on the take-off side without any rail, hedge, or ditch in front of them.

A *spread fence* or obstacle is one that requires the horse to jump width as well as height. The most common spread fence is the *oxer*. There are two kinds of oxers, the *ascending* and the *square*. In the *ascending oxer* the first element of the fence is lower than the second, creating a step-like appearance. It is desirable to have at least 6 to 9 inches' difference between the first and second elements of the obstacle. The *square oxer,* in which the top rails of the two elements are of the same height, is more difficult to jump and not legal in hunter competition. A *triple bar* is a spread fence with three elements in ascending order. A *hog's back* is a spread fence with the front and rear elements lower than the center element. The *width* of a spread fence is measured from the two outermost top extremities on a line parallel to the ground. Care should be taken not to have a solid element or more than one or two poles forming the rear element of a spread fence.

Banks, slopes, ramps, or *sunken roads* in a course in the ring are regarded as combinations of obstacles. The course designer must decide if they are *closed* or *open combinations*. A combination is *closed* if the horse cannot get out without jumping.

A *water jump* is a spread obstacle that must not have any other obstacle before, in the middle, or beyond the ditch full of water. It may have a guardrail or hedge, fixed to the ground and not more than 2½ feet high, on the take-off side. The guardrail or hedge is not considered part of the obstacle for the purpose of judging faults, although it is included in the calculation of the total width of the obstacle. The limits of water jumps without guardrails or hedges must be clearly marked both on the take-off and the landing sides, usually by a white strip of wood or other suitable material; if there is a rail or hedge on the take-off side, such marking is needed only on the landing side. Under certain conditions AHSA rules allow a water jump to have a rail over the middle no more than 3 feet 6 inches in height.

Combinations occur when two, three, or more fences are placed one after the other, not more than 39 feet 5 inches apart, and require one, two, or more successive jumping efforts. They are treated differently under the special rules for show jumping, hunters, and equitation. Distances between fences in combination should be at least 23 feet in horse classes and 20 feet in pony classes. The distance between fences in combination is measured from the base of the fence on the landing side to the base of the next fence on the take-off side. Obviously in the case of cross-country obstacles, the nature of the terrain and the approximate place where the average horse will land and take off as a result must be taken into consideration.

A horse in approaching a fence judges the point at which he intends to take off by looking at the line of the base of the obstacle. Thus the bottom of the fence is the *ground line*. Since a horse is inclined to take off from a point too close to or underneath a fence, an obstacle can be made more jumpable if the ground line is slightly in advance of the main part of the obstacle by the addition of a rail, flower box, hedge, and so forth. In all cases a *false ground line* must be avoided, that is, one that causes a horse to misjudge where to take off to jump the obstacle. Good ground lines are important in competitions for novice horses and riders and also in advanced competitions where the horse is expected to jump great heights and spreads.

Conversion Table of Yards, Feet, and Meters

1 inch	=	0.025 m.		1.00 m.	=	3 ft. 3.37 ins.
1 foot	=	0.305 m.		1.10 m.	=	3 ft. 7.25 ins.
2 ft.	=	0.61 m.		1.20 m.	=	3 ft. 11.25 ins.
2 ft. 6 ins.	=	0.79 m.		1.30 m.	=	4 ft. 3 ins.
1 yard	=	0.91 m.		1.40 m.	=	4 ft. 7 ins.
3 ft. 7 ins.	=	1.10 m.		1.50 m.	=	4 ft. 11 ins.
3 ft. 11 ins.	=	1.20 m.		1.60 m.	=	5 ft. 3 ins.
4 ft.	=	1.22 m.		1.70 m.	=	5 ft. 7 ins.
4 ft. 3 ins.	=	1.30 m.		1.80 m.	=	5 ft. 11 ins.
4 ft. 5 ins.	=	1.35 m.		1.90 m.	=	6 ft. 3 ins.
4 ft. 6 ins.	=	1.37 m.		2.00 m.	=	6 ft. 7 ins.
4 ft. 7 ins.	=	1.40 m.		3.00 m.	=	9 ft. 10 ins.
4 ft. 9 ins.	=	1.45 m.		4.00 m.	=	13 ft. 1 ins.
5 ft.	=	1.52 m.		5.00 m.	=	16 ft. 5 ins.
5 ft. 3 ins.	=	1.60 m.		6.00 m.	=	19 ft. 8 ins.
5 ft. 6 ins.	=	1.68 m.		7.00 m.	=	22 ft. 11 ins.
5 ft. 11 ins.	=	1.80 m.		8.00 m.	=	26 ft. 3 ins.
6 ft.	=	1.83 m.		9.00 m.	=	29 ft. 6 ins.
6 ft. 6 ins.	=	1.91 m.		10.00 m.	=	32 ft. 10 ins.
7 ft.	=	2.13 m.		25.00 m.	=	82 ft.
7 ft. 2 ins.	=	2.20 m.		100.00 m.	=	109.3 yds.
8 ft.	=	2.44 m.		1000.00 m.	=	1093.6 yds.
8 ft. 2 ins.	=	2.50 m.		1600.00 m.	=	1749.8 yds.
9 ft.	=	2.74 m.				
9 ft. 2 ins.	=	2.80 m.				
9 ft. 10 ins.	=	3.00 m.				
10 ft.	=	3.05 m.				
11 ft. 8 ins.	=	3.50 m.				
13 ft. 1 ins.	=	4.00 m.				
15 ft.	=	4.57 m.				
20 ft.	=	6.10 m.				
10 yds.	=	9.14 m.				
25 yds.	=	22.86 m.				
50 yds.	=	45.72 m.				
100 yds.	=	91.44 m.				
1000 yds.	=	914.40 m.				
1760 yds.	=	1609.30 m.				

For practical purposes one kilometer is considered to be 5/8 of a mile and 1600 meters is one mile.

For more accuracy: 1 meter = 3.281 feet
Multiply number of feet by 0.3048 to get number of meters
Multiply number of meters by .0006214 to get number of miles